Managing Purchasing

Sourcing and contracting

Andrew Erridge

For Colette and Mark

Butterworth-Heinemann Ltd
Linacre House, Jordan Hill, Oxford OX2 8DP

℞ A member of the Reed Elsevier plc group

OXFORD LONDON BOSTON
MUNICH NEW DELHI SINGAPORE SYDNEY
TOKYO TORONTO WELLINGTON

First published 1995

British Library Cataloguing in Publication Data
Erridge, Andrew
  Managing Purchasing: Sourcing and
  Contracting
  I. Title
  658.72

ISBN 0 7506 1941 4

Typeset by Keyword Typesetting Services Ltd, Wallington, Surrey
Printed and bound in Great Britain

Managing Purchasing

2004

The Chartered Institute of Purchasing and Supply is the centre of excellence in all matters relating to procurement and supply chain management. It is the central reference point worldwide for this significant management process – a process with an annual 'spend' in excess of £750bn in the UK alone.

The Chartered Institute's range of services reflects the professional requirements of individuals and their employers – public or private, large or small.

For a free information pack please contact:

The Chartered Institute of Purchasing and Supply
Easton House
Easton on the Hill
Stamford
Lincolnshire
PE9 3NZ

Tel: 01780 56777
Fax: 01780 51610

Contents

Acknowledgements

In writing this book I have benefitted from the co-operation, advice and help of many people too numerous to mention by name. First, all those who were interviewed as part of the research for the development of the Purchasing Standards, as well as their employers for allowing their busy work schedules to be interrupted.

Next, the members of the Purchasing and Supply Lead Body, who supported the idea of the book collectively and individually with words of encouragement. I would especially like to thank Will Reid, Lead Body Secretary, for his assistance.

John Plant of Rolls Royce Aerospace, and Rod Brooke of British Telecom acted as referees for the book, and their constructive comments were invaluable. Gareth Jones of the Department of Transport 'road tested' a draft of the book and contributed greatly to its clarity and accuracy in relation to public procurement.

I would also like to thank my colleagues at the University of Ulster, especially Shayne Perry, Phil Willett and Graham Cowan, for their direct and indirect contributions to the text. My appreciation is also due to staff of Government Purchasing Service in Northern Ireland, some of whose real world experience of purchasing tempered my more theoretical approach to the book.

My apologies to the many students on Purchasing and Supply Management courses at the University of Ulster who suffered early versions of some of the material included in the book.

Special thanks are due to Mavis Wilson who helped with the preparation of the text.

Finally, and most importantly, I would like to thank my wife Colette for her absolute support and encouragement, without which the book could not have been written.

Introduction

The primary purpose of this book is to provide the essential knowledge and understanding for candidates undertaking assessment against the purchasing standards developed by the Purchasing and Supply Lead Body (PSLB). These form the basis for the National Vocational Qualifications (NVQs) and Scottish Vocational Qualifications (SVQs) in purchasing, and they may also be used by organizations for their own staff development. The purchasing standards are part of a suite of standards for the supply chain being developed by the Purchasing and Supply and other Lead Bodies. Other relevant sets of standards already developed or undergoing development include:

- Inventory Management (PSLB).
- Materials Management (PSLB).
- Contract Management (PSLB).
- Warehousing and Wholesaling (National Wholesale Training Council).
- International Trade and Services (International Trade and Services Lead Body).

Whilst it is clear that all these functions are linked in the supply chain concept which is discussed in Chapter 1, the scope of this book is restricted to the core purchasing functions covered by the purchasing standards, although where appropriate reference is made to linkages with other functions in the supply chain.

The book is entitled *Managing Purchasing*, although there are no generic management units within the purchasing NVQs and SVQs. The sense in which the book is about managing purchasing is in terms of managing external resources, to use Richard Lamming's phrase. Those resources are principally supply markets and suppliers, both actual and potential, and the supply chain through which flow the goods and services necessary for the organization to operate. In order to manage these resources efficiently and effectively, the purchaser requires sets of competences and knowledge. The purchasing NVQs and SVQs represent an authoritative statement of the competences and knowledge required, built around the core purchasing tasks of sourcing and contracting. Managing these tasks efficiently and effectively requires a thorough knowledge of, and the ability to translate into practice, a wide range of theories and techniques, which this book aims to present in an accessible, practical manner.

The book is therefore written for all staff performing the buying role, either as their full-time work or as part of a wider range of roles. Those who in addition have managerial or supervisory responsibilities, for whom general management qualifications would be appropriate, are already well provided for by texts in Butterworth-Heinemann's Institute of Management series on *Managing Financial Resources*, *The Management Task*, *Personal Effectiveness* and *Managing People* (see References and further reading). The competences and knowledge underlying general management are therefore not dealt with in this book.

Purchasing NVQs and SVQs have been developed for Levels 2, 3 and 4 of the NCVQ framework. The units and levels are set out in Table I.1, together with the chapters in this book in which the knowledge requirements are covered. This book is designed to cover all three levels, although clearly the knowledge required at each level will differ. The rationale for this is that, firstly, there will be many candidates who will wish to progress through the levels and, secondly, the proactive, creative buyer for whom the book is written will wish to extend his or her knowledge beyond that of direct relevance to the level of qualification for which they are currently registered.

Each chapter relates to at least one NVQ or SVQ unit, and presents an overview of relevant theory and practice. Within each chapter there is also the opportunity for you to explore practical cases, to investigate issues in relation to your own organization, and to complete activities relating to the knowledge and competences covered. The questions are designed to encourage you to review and revise the material covered in each chapter. The activities in particular provide the opportunity for you to produce written work which may be suitable for submission as evidence against NVQ or SVQ assessment, or as coursework for professional or academic courses.

In addition to covering the knowledge requirements for the purchasing NVQs and SVQs, this book is intended to be of value to students enrolled on courses leading to the Chartered Institute of Purchasing and Supply (CIPS) qualifications as well as Business and Technology Education Council and degree courses. The revised CIPS syllabuses for which it is suggested the book is appropriate, either in full or in part, are:

- Purchasing.
- Commercial Relationships.
- Purchasing and Supply Chain Management I: Strategy.
- Purchasing and Supply Chain Management II: Tactics and Operations.

NCVQ requirements for standards development

At this point it is important to note a number of features of standards development as prescribed by the National Council for Vocational Qualifications (NCVQ) which impact on the selection and presentation of the material incorporated in this book.

Table I.1
Purchasing NVQs and SVQs: levels and chapters

Unit No.	Unit title	Level 2	Level 3	Level 4	Chap. No.
001	Contributing to the health and safety of the working environment	*	*	*	NA
002	Creating and maintaining appropriate professional relationships	*	*	*	NA
003	Contributing to the installation and improvement of purchasing related systems	*			NA
004	Establishing and operating a database of purchasing/stores information	*			NA
005	Communicating to maintain supplier performance	*			6
006	Acquiring specified supplies	*			8
007	Progressing the delivery of supplies	*			9
008	Contributing to the maintenance of systems for security and confidentiality	*	*	*	NA
009	Telecommunications and data transmission	*			NA
010	Contributing to organizational strategy		*	*	1
011	Determining supplier performance and continuity of supply		*		6
012	Contributing to the establishment and evaluation of current and future requirements for supply		*		7
013	Maintaining the effectiveness of purchasing operations		*		10
014	Selecting supplier for specific supplies		*	*	8
015	Contracting for supply		*	*	9
016	Contributing to the establishment and improvement of purchasing related systems		*		NA
017	Establishing and maintaining a database of purchasing/stores information		*		NA
018	Negotiating improvements in supplier performance		*		6
019	Determining the conditions in the market for suppliers			*	2
020	Determining potential suppliers through vendor evaluation			*	3
021	Optimizing the supplier base			*	4
022	Entering into strategic sourcing arrangements			*	5
023	Contributing to the establishment and integration of purchasing related systems			*	NA
024	Establishing and maintaining a database of purchasing/stores and management information			*	NA
025	Obtaining improvements in supplier performance			*	6
026	Establishing and evaluating current and future requirements for supply			*	7
027	Developing the effectiveness of purchasing operations			*	10

*Compulsory for this level.
NA, not applicable.

Accessibility

The qualifications must be accessible to any candidate in the UK wishing to undergo assessment. Therefore the standards must reflect practice which is representative of the majority of organizations, rather than those which are world class. This is because the candidate in an organization which is less than world class may not be able to access parts of the qualification if they do not have the facilities or opportunity to demonstrate competence against some of the Units. Thus whilst organizations with world-class purchasing functions may be practising strategic partnership and supplier development, these cannot be made compulsory for all candidates. Despite this constraint, however, strategic purchasing approaches and concepts have been embedded in the standards in a way which should enable anybody employed in the purchasing function to demonstrate competence by testing of knowledge, if not by practice. They are also therefore reflected in this book, particularly from the critical perspective of the purchaser who needs to be aware of not only the claimed benefits of practices such as partnership, but also of the costs and disadvantages, and means of successful implementation.

Similarly, the standards, as well as the book, are designed to cover in a balanced manner the purchase of both goods and services. There is an increasing change of emphasis across all sectors, but not least in the public sector, from goods to services. Whilst many aspects of sourcing and contracting are the same or very similar, some, in particular specification, evaluation of offers and contract monitoring, differ in their degree of complexity and the consequent demands on the purchaser. Such areas of difference are highlighted in the text and, where appropriate, cases and examples are used to illustrate the purchase of services.

Size of organization, cross-sectoral and national coverage

The research on which the standards were based was required to involve companies of various sizes, from different sectors and locations throughout the UK, so as not to embody practices specific to any particular type of organization. Size of organization is significant in that larger organizations will tend to be more departmentalized, and therefore candidates from such organizations may not be able to access some of the units within the qualifications. On the other hand, candidates from small companies may be responsible not only for purchasing but for other functions as well. Thus the standards were drafted to reflect the range of tasks considered essential for a candidate to be accepted as competent in purchasing, rather than what any individual buyer in a specific organization is expected to do. Again there is provision in the standards for assessment of knowledge if it is not possible to provide practical evidence of competence.

In respect of sectors, there are major differences between purchasing practice in the public sector and the utilities covered by the EC Procurement Directives, and practice in parts of the private sector, for example the automotive industry. In particular, this relates to the development of partnership relationships, and the selection of suppliers, with a more competitive, adversarial approach prescribed by legislation and procedures. This led to a debate as to whether tendering was an area of competence against which all purchasers should be assessed. It was decided that this should be the case, on the basis that whether or not a particular organization carried out tendering, it provided a set of procedures and a discipline in which all purchasers should be competent, and should be able to determine for themselves its strengths and weaknesses. Allied to this is the possibility of mobility of staff between the sectors, where the new employer may require competence in tendering. Tendering is therefore covered at some length in this text, especially given its increasing use in buying services.

Location of the organization was found not to be significant in the standards research, and so the standards reflect practice which is common not only throughout the UK, but to an increasing extent on a European and North American basis. Ideas of strategic purchasing have clearly been strongly influenced, however, by Japanese practice, which has been found not to be transferable in its entirety beyond the context of governmental support, integrated supplier networks and just-in-time kanban delivery systems unique to Japan (Lamming, 1993; Oliver and Hunter, 1994). This again emphasized the need to ensure that the standards were based on a model which was appropriate to the context within which the majority of purchasers in the UK work, which is reflected in the approach adopted in this book.

Subject to review

The purchasing NVQs were approved in November 1992 and, as with all NVQs, are subject to review after three years. At this stage, the content of some units and elements may be changed, as may the overall qualification structure. Whilst the competences recognized as essential to become qualified in purchasing are unlikely to change substantially, their expression in terms of performance criteria, range statements and knowledge and evidence requirements is likely to be amended on review.

Therefore this book does not follow the NVQ or SVQ units and elements verbatim, but aims to cover the knowledge requirements for each unit broadly. It is unlikely, therefore, that the relevance of the book to the purchasing NVQs and SVQs will be significantly reduced as a result of their review, although the order of presentation and numbering of units may change slightly from that presented in Table I.1. The wording of titles of units and elements may also change slightly, but they are unlikely to differ substantially from those currently included in the qualifications.

Knowledge requirements

Assessment of knowledge for NVQs and SVQs is required to cover the minimum necessary for competence to be demonstrated. It does not therefore cover as extensive an area as the traditional syllabus for an academic or professional course of study. Thus the knowledge requirements identified in the standards are necessarily fairly sparse, and focused very directly on the performance of the competence rather than the analysis of competing theories or the balancing of evidence to reach a valid conclusion. However, partly because the book is also written to be of use to students on traditional courses of study as well as those registered for NVQs or SVQs, and partly because the author's academic pretensions are hard to escape, the book ranges much wider and deeper than a strict reading of the Standards would dictate. A wider and deeper coverage of knowledge requirements based upon current research will also ensure that the book does not quickly become out of date, or less relevant following the review of the NVQs and SVQs. In fact, the qualifications and their knowledge requirements are likely to be amended in order to 'catch up' with the developments in theory and practice reflected in this book.

Ultimately, my view is that demonstration of both knowledge and practical competence, preferably in an integrated manner, is essential for the achievement of both professional and academic qualifications, though with differing degrees of attainment. This approach is endorsed in an Employment Department Briefing Paper on knowledge and understanding (Mitchell and Bartram, 1994) which recommends that testing of both performance and knowledge is essential to ensure competence against each element within an NVQ or SVQ.

Non-purchasing units

Within the purchasing NVQs and SVQs, there are general units, variants of which are featured in many qualifications. These cover:

- Health and safety.
- Maintaining professional relationships with others.
- Establishing and integrating systems.
- Establishing and operating a database.
- Maintaining security and confidentiality.
- Data transmission.

These aspects are not dealt with directly in this book, as they do not draw on any specific expertise in or knowledge of purchasing. However, useful sources of information and guidance on these units are identified in the References and further reading section at the end of this chapter.

Research and other sources

The primary source material on which this book is based is the research which was carried out in the course of the development of the purchasing standards. This involved a series of interviews in twenty four organizations, including twelve manufacturing companies, three public sector organizations and nine service companies. Organizations were selected to ensure that the total included those of large, medium and small size, and from various geographical locations throughout the UK (see Erridge and Perry (1993) for a fuller account of the research and the resulting standards). This was to ensure that the standards would not be based on organizations of a single type, but would reflect the wide range of circumstances under which purchasing staff do their jobs. Those interviewed included staff at various levels: directors of purchasing, purchasing managers, buyers of various grades, and purchasing assistants. This ensured that the standards did not merely reflect the tasks performed by staff at a particular level and, by including senior staff, afforded an insight into strategic aspects of purchasing which are reflected in the standards and in this book.

A wide range of secondary sources have also been drawn upon, mainly textbooks and research based texts as well as academic articles for theoretical perspectives, and professional journals for practical cases. The case material is selected to illustrate particular approaches embedded in the standards, and is not claimed to be representative or generalizable. The case studies are intended to provide you with the opportunity to assess theory against practice, and to test whether your own experience is similar to or differs from that in the cases described. The questions in the text are designed to encourage you to reflect upon these issues, rather than just to accept theory or a case report at face value. It is hoped therefore that your critical faculties will be stimulated by the questions and activities found in each chapter, and that by reflecting upon your own experience you will develop an independent view of purchasing practice which is more than sufficient to achieve the qualification on which you are engaged.

References and further reading

Erridge, A. and Perry, S. (1993) *National Standards of Competence: Purchasing*, Chartered Institute of Purchasing and Supply, Easton on the Hill

Lamming, R. (1993) *Beyond Partnership: Strategies for Innovation and Lean Supply*, Prentice Hall, Hemel Hempstead

Mitchell, L. and Bartram, D. (1994) *The Place of Knowledge and Understanding in the Development of National Vocational Qualifications and Scottish Vocational Qualifications (Competence and Assessment Briefing Series No. 10)*, Employment Department, Pendragon Press, Papworth Everard

Oliver, N. and Hunter, G. (1994) *The Financial Impact of Japanese Production Methods in UK Companies (Research Papers in Management Studies No. 24)*, University of Cambridge, Cambridge

Sources for non-purchasing units

Broadbent, M. and Cullen, J. (1993) *Managing Financial Resources*, Butterworth-Heinemann, Oxford

Dixon, R. (1993) *The Management Task*, Butterworth-Heinemann, Oxford

French, C. S. (1993) *Data Processing and Information Technology*, 9th edn, DP Publications, London

Health and Safety Executive (1993) *A Step by Step Guide to COSHH Assessment*, HMSO, London

Health and Safety Executive (1994) *Essentials of Health and Safety at Work*, HSE Books, Sudbury, Suffolk
Murdock, A. and Scutt, C. (1993) *Personal Effectiveness*, Butterworth-Heinemann, Oxford
Thomson, R. (1993) *Managing People*, Butterworth-Heinemann, Oxford
Wilson, D. A. (1993) *Managing Information*, Butterworth-Heinemann, Oxford

PART ONE

The Supply Chain

1 The supply chain concept

Introduction

The main purpose of this chapter is to demonstrate that how we practise purchasing depends very much upon how we think about the purchasing process. If we think about purchasing as a largely self-contained, clerical function, then our aims and assessment of its effectiveness will relate solely to processes internal to the department, such as how many orders we process in a given period of time. If, however, we think of purchasing as part of a more extended strategic process, usually referred to as the 'supply chain', then other factors become more important, such as how we link the purchasing process to other functions, and how we manage the overall process of acquiring goods and services for the organization.

The objectives of this chapter are therefore to:

● Examine models of the purchasing process.
● Introduce supply chain concepts.
● Identify links between purchasing and other functions in the supply chain.
● Explore the strategic contribution of purchasing.
● Present the model on which this book is based.

The purchasing process

A typical purchasing process is presented below. It comprises the following stages.

Requisition

The person requiring goods completes a form, either manually or, as is increasingly the case, electronically, obtains the necessary authorization, and forwards the requisition to purchasing.

Checking the requisition

The buyer checks that the requisition is properly authorized, is charged to the correct budget code, and that it is correctly specified. The specification could be either a product name and type, or a more complex description of what is required either in words or drawings.

Selecting a supplier

The buyer identifies one or more possible suppliers through various means including:

- Catalogues.
- Previous purchases.
- Existing contracts.

Most organizations have rules governing how many quotations should be obtained in relation to the value of the order. In ascending order of value, the following may be required:

- Telephone quotes from three sources.
- Written quotes from three sources.
- Advertise for bids in local newspapers.

Once the quotes or bids have been obtained, the buyer selects a supplier who can meet the specification, usually on the basis of price.

Ordering

The buyer completes an order, stating the location to which the goods are to be delivered, and by when, if appropriate. The order is sent to the supplier, again either manually or electronically.

Expediting

In some organizations, it is the responsibility of the purchasing department to monitor the deliveries from the suppliers, to liaise with goods inward staff and to match delivery notes with orders. The account can then be passed to the finance department for payment.

This is a very straightforward process with the following characteristics:

- Clerical, emphasizing speed and accuracy of processing requisitions and orders.
- Reactive, responding to requisitioners and suppliers passively.
- Little direct communications or negotiation with requisitioners or suppliers.
- Rule bound, following procedures designed to ensure that the organization's money is being spent for legitimate purposes.

Such a process, if carried out efficiently, should ensure that the organization obtains the goods it needs within a reasonable time-scale and at the price set by the market, which may or may not be competitive. The success of the purchasing department may be assessed by:

- The speed with which orders are processed: though this does not guarantee that the orders were necessary.
- Whether the organization spends its budget within the financial year: though this does not guarantee that the spend was either necessary or best value for money.
- Availability of goods: though this does not guarantee that the right quantity of goods is available only for the period of time they are required.
- Quality performance of goods: though this is more dependent on the accuracy of specification by the requisitioner than the buyer's own input, and does not guarantee that the quality standard is not set too high for the performance requirements.

Thus if we think about, or conceptualize, the purchasing process as it is presented above, the organization may have a very efficient purchasing department which is actually costing a considerable amount of money by its inability, if not failure, to adopt a more proactive approach to sourcing the organization's requirements.

A proactive approach would emphasize the following features:

- Joint responsibility of users and purchasers for agreeing specifications.
- Active analysis of market conditions to assess the competitiveness of prices quoted.
- Pre-supply assessment and continuous monitoring of supply performance by current and potential suppliers.
- Negotiation with suppliers to obtain the most beneficial mix of conditions of supply, i.e. price, quantity, quality, delivery and payment terms.
- Analysis of the supply base to reduce the number of suppliers and improve the quality of those remaining, thereby reducing the number of different supplier administrative procedures with which the organization has to deal, and consequently reducing the number of separate files the organization needs to maintain.

This book is based upon such a strategic, proactive conceptualization of the purchasing process, which will be outlined in more detail at the end of this chapter.

The supply chain

As a buyer, you will have a good knowledge of your immediate suppliers and internal customers, the people on whose behalf you purchase goods and services. However, how well do you know your suppliers' own suppliers, or the source of the raw materials, parts or subassemblies which go into the products or support the services you purchase? In a reactive role, the buyer would simply accept the prices offered by potential suppliers, without consideration of the costs which contribute to those prices. As you will be aware from your own organization, bought-in goods and services contribute between 50% and 80% of the total costs of most organizations. If this is true for your organization, it is also true for your suppliers, and their suppliers, and so on back along the chain. Thus it is important that you understand the supply chain for your own organization, and, together with your most important immediate suppliers, seek to adopt methods of purchasing which reduce cost and improve quality throughout the chain.

A simple model of the supply chain for a manufacturing company is presented in Figure 1.1. The first link in the chain is the raw materials extractor, e.g. the oil company whose crude oil will be transported to a refinery and then be used either to produce energy in the form of electricity to power the production line, or will fuel the company's own generators or heating system; or will provide the fuel for the transport of supplies and finished products. Alternatively, aluminium cylinder heads originate as bauxite, which is then processed into aluminium, machined into a cylinder head, and supplied to the final assembler or manufacturer. Some raw materials will be purchased direct by the final assembler or manufacturer, whilst their suppliers will also buy in those raw materials required for their part of the manufacturing process.

At each stage in the supply chain, there are the purchasing activities of supplier selection and contracting, as well as transport and delivery, and in most cases storage, which are generally the responsibility of other departments. However, the buyer is responsible for ensuring that the costs of the overall purchase are taken into account, including purchase price, transport, delivery and storage, as well as quality and a host of other factors which will be explored in later chapters. Thus buyers throughout the supply chain have the opportunity, if not the responsibility, to examine carefully the cost structure of their most significant purchases. Increasingly, if you are a supplier to a major manufacturer, this is information which is being 'shared', or at worst demanded by the manufacturer before you are given the business. If you are expected to have this information, and to be able to reduce your own purchase costs, then it makes sense to require the same discipline of your own suppliers.

Figure 1.2 illustrates the supply chain for the retail sector (Department of Trade and Industry 1991, p.2). This demonstrates the importance of packaging for products which are for resale rather than internal consumption, and also the complexity of the distribution chain. In this context the buyer's main

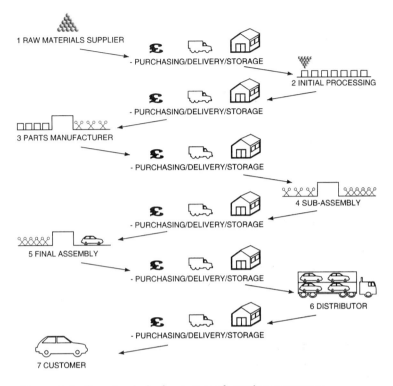

Figure 1.1 Supply chain for a manufacturing company

concern may be for the attractiveness of the product to the consumer, within a fixed retail price which determines the scope for negotiation with suppliers and distributors.

The supply chain for a service contract may be even more extended, in that the buyer has to consider not only the quality, frequency, price, etc., of the service to be delivered, but also the products and services which the contractor will be using. For example, the quality and cost of a catering contractor's service will be significantly affected by the ingredients purchased, the method of storing and cooking the food, the staff employed, etc. All these factors may need to be examined in assessing bids, and the source of the supplies and services may need to be investigated and become the subject of negotiation before a contract is awarded.

Whilst the buyer's main interaction and contribution is upstream along the supply chain, there is also an important liaison function with those downstream: the immediate customer and their customers. This may happen directly, through participation in a major customer's supplier development activities or, more likely, indirectly through interaction with your own organization's sales and marketing staff, or the internal customers whose specification of their requirements will reflect the needs of your external customers downstream. Therefore it is important to consider relationships with staff of other departments within your own organization.

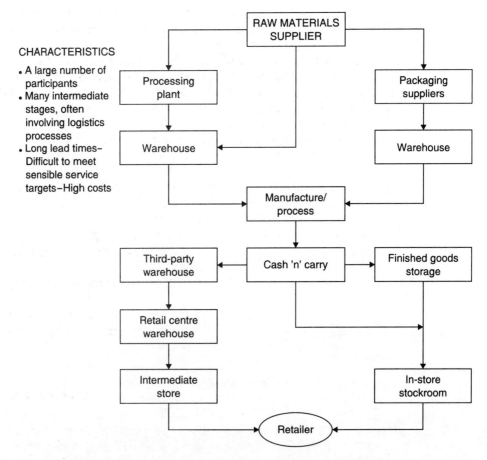

CHARACTERISTICS

- A large number of participants
- Many intermediate stages, often involving logistics processes
- Long lead times– Difficult to meet sensible service targets–High costs

Figure 1.2 Traditional food and drink industry supply chain. (From Department of Trade and Industry, *Logistics and Supply Chain Management, Management in the '90s*, HMSO, London, 1991)

Integration with other functions

Barriers to effective performance within the supply chain are often perceived as being at the boundaries of the organizations within the chain, i.e. between suppliers and their customers. However, a further set of barriers is identified by Syson (1992), those between the various departments involved in the supply chain within the organization. Syson distinguishes between the Interface Model of the traditional supply chain, and the Integrated Model of the ideal supply chain, and identifies forces of change which make it important for organizations to move from the former to the latter.

The Interface Model is characterized by 'the presence of well-defined organizational boundaries with inconsistent policies being pursued in each area and with independent control systems' (p. 84). It has the following features:

- *Organizational divisions*: each part of the supply chain is under different 'ownership'; each building in security through higher forecasts and longer lead times.
- *Inconsistent policies*: policies may actually conflict e.g. needs of stores and production for high stock levels against the cost of financing stock; independent control systems; separately developed software for each part of the chain.
- *Staged inventories*: maximization of purchase inventory, work in progress and stocks of finished goods to satisfy the needs of each separate 'division'.

He identifies a number of 'forces for change' which have made the Interface Model inappropriate:

- The need for sustainable competitive advantage
- Global competition, with the spread of industrialization, and suppliers as a source of cost reduction
- Economic changes, including recession and increased competition for supply
- Technological change, with shorter product life cycles, the increasing cost and complexity of products, lean production, Just-in-Time and Electronic Data Interchange
- The importance of 'green' purchasing
- A trend to the purchase of services
- An increasing proportion of bought-in goods and services as a percentage of total resources expended

These forces of change have resulted in the need for a new Ideal Supply Chain model based upon integration. This is characterized by 'not only a strategic overview of the entire chain, but also operational control of the different segments and the ability to make trade-offs in one part of the chain in order to maximize benefits elsewhere' (p. 88). Its features are:

- The supply chain is a single entity, integrated at different levels of management: strategic, planning and operational
- Supply moves centre stage, and is a shared objective of all functions
- Inventories are a last resort: the question 'why is it there?' needs to be asked, not 'how much?'
- Systems are integrated, with real time data flow, and shared ownership of information

INVESTIGATE

- *Can you identify the flows within your supply chain, especially those within your own organization? Are they characterized better by the interface model or the integrated model? Can you identify the departments or functions with which you interact most frequently and significantly?*

You may have identified any or all of the following functions with which you may be involved more or less frequently:

- Research and design.
- Production.
- Engineering.
- Other customer departments, e.g. office staff.
- Sales and marketing.
- Quality.
- Stores.
- Information technology.
- Materials management.
- Inventory management.
- Finance.
- Transport and delivery.
- Accounts.
- Legal.

Not all organizations will have all of the above functions, but in principle the buyer's role requires a concern for, and interaction with, all these aspects of the overall business or service provided. At one level, the buyer is responsible for selecting a supplier and contracting for all goods and services to support these activities. This is the core task, or competence, and therefore it is essential that it is performed efficiently and effectively if purchasing is to be seen as a key contributor to the overall performance of the organization. In performing these core tasks, buyers will need to advise and consult with the following:

- *Supplier selection*: to choose the supplier(s) offering the best combination of price, quality, quantity, delivery and overall performance in conjunction with production, engineering, quality, marketing, stores, transport and delivery, inventory management and materials management.
- *Contract for supply*: to establish the best terms for the supply balancing risks and costs to the organization and its suppliers, in conjunction with production, accounts, legal, stores, transport and delivery, inventory management, materials management.

However, to perform the task proactively, purchasing needs to liaise with staff from other functions across a wider range of activities:

- *Identifying needs*: to examine strategic issues such as make or buy, new product areas, new markets, new materials, in conjunction with internal customers, e.g. production, engineering, service delivery departments, marketing and finance.
- *Specification*: to establish the performance and physical character- istics of the goods and services to be purchased, in conjunction with research and design, internal customers, marketing and quality.
- *Storage, transport and delivery (logistics)*: to establish the optimum strategy for stock and its movement from supplier to the organiza- tion and to its customers, both internal and external, possibly invol- ving reductions in levels and locations of stores, smaller, more frequent deliveries to point of use at the times required (just-in- time), in conjunction with quality, stores, materials management, inventory management, finance, transport and delivery.

In many organizations a team approach is being adopted, with buyers participating with engineers and designers to the identification and specifi- cation of requirements, and with inventory and materials specialists in the design and management of logistics.

The range of responsibilities of a Purchasing Director in a manufacturing company is demonstrated opposite.

Integration of purchasing and logistics

I am responsible for purchasing ingredients, packaging, including design and marketing content, machinery and equipment. I am also responsible for logistics, i.e. planning of sales, despatch, com- municating with production, agreeing systems, receiving the fac- tory plans and transport plans, making sure they are all integrated and make sense, and measuring performance against plans. Essentially my role is to make sure that the right stock is in the right place at the right time, and that there is a balance between forecasts, input of materials and output. Whilst I do not take execu- tive responsibility for stores, I lay down the ground rules, agree objectives, improve operations in conjunction with distribution and production's finished goods stores. My major responsibility is supply chain management.

Source: Interview, Purchasing and Logistics Director, Nestlé Rowntree

---

At this senior level, clearly responsibility for various functions is drawn together. At lower levels between the various departments mentioned, i.e.

purchasing, production, distribution, stores, etc., there is a need for co-ordination, interaction and integration of plans.

Customer service

Whilst the buyer's principal business relationship is with the supplier, the importance of the internal customer, the person or department on whose behalf the goods or services are being sourced, has to be recognized. The concept of purchasing as a service department, an overhead whose costs can only be justified in terms of the savings or quality improvements obtained through effective and efficient sourcing, is one which should help to focus attention on the importance of providing a quality service to the internal customer. However, the support and co-operation of internal customers may not be immediately given. This may be because purchasing is seen as:

- Imposing procedures which are regarded as unnecessary or cumbersome.
- Coming between an internal customer and a preferred supplier.
- Inadequately qualified to comment on overall requirements or particular specifications.
- Contributing to cost but not to value.

Such resentment or resistance to the involvement of purchasing should be overcome, not by an equal and opposite reaction, but by earning the customers' goodwill and respect through improved performance. The case study based on Glaxo below sets out how this may be achieved.

Added value through purchasing in Glaxo

Peter Garnett, former Purchasing Director, outlines the characteristics of purchasing before and after reorganization. Before reorganization, the function was characterized by the following features:

- It added to cost, not value, with £2.5 million per year direct and indirect labour costs, documentation, communications, accommodation, warehousing, stock, etc.
- It was a paper based, clerical function, placing orders.
- There were high administration costs per order: 60% of orders were for less than £250, 25% for less than £50.
- There was an emphasis on price, with targets based on savings and variance from budget.
- There were too many suppliers (more than 4500), and 27 for stationery.
- The knock-on costs were high, with finance staff checking and matching invoices against goods received notes.
- The purchasing manual was unread!

- The function was hierarchical, with six grades.
- In behavioural terms, the approach was win/lose, confrontational, and emphasized departmentalism.

'Purchasing was however seen as successful within its niche of obtaining goods on time, being price aggressive, and . . . coping with the administrative burden' (Garnett, 1992, p. 5).

After reorganization, purchasing has become a strategic function, with the following success factors:

- A reduced supplier base: 80% of spend is with 30 suppliers, and 60% with 10 suppliers.
- Continuous improvement through supplier development.
- Long-term partnerships.
- Zero lead time.
- Electronic transfer of information – from supplier production to Glaxo stock.
- Reduced costs of low value orders through allowing variances in paperwork, faxing orders, and electronic requisitioning.

Garnett outlines the following methods through which this increase in purchasing's added value was achieved:

- The use of procurement positioning to understand the risk/cost model and the resulting activity spread (see Purchasing portfolio analysis in Chapter 4).
- Uncoupling operational and strategic purchasing groups.
- Reducing resource cost by removing purchasing activity, people and processes which do not add value.
- Managing risk through continuous strategies to overcome profit exposure from supply interruption.
- Making the best use of people through minimizing transactional processes, and introducing new skills, e.g. strategic thinkers and supplier development managers.
- Removing waste in the process, and continuously seeking improvement.

Source: Garnett, P. (1992) Adding Value through the Purchasing Function, *CIPS Conference, Solihull, October*

INVESTIGATE

- *To which of the above set of characteristics, before or after, does your organization conform more closely? If it is the former, are there ways in which you can reduce waste and increase the focus on value-adding activities? How useful are the methods Garnett outlines in achieving value added purchasing in your organization?*

Purchasing as a strategic function

Purchasing's claim to play a strategic role in organizations may be said to rest on its contribution to making the most efficient and effective matching of resources to markets, customers or clients through its management of a critical element of the external environment, namely the organization's supply base.

From being a separate, subordinate department, purchasing is increasingly seen as part of an integrated approach to the supply of goods and services through its relationships with suppliers. Lamming's (1993) concept of 'external resource management' encapsulates the perception of suppliers and their assets as an extension of organizational resources, the management of which represents purchasing's strategic contribution.

Pearson and Gritzmacher (1990) identify the following factors which enhance purchasing's strategic role:

- The supply environment, the effective management of which can lead to added value and greater integration of supply and marketing strategies.
- The intense level of competition resulting in increasing concern for product quality through collaboration with suppliers.
- A change in the role of purchasing from simply cost cutting to profit generating.

The emphasis on high product quality was perceived to be at the heart of the success of Japanese manufacturing industry. Externally, this was based on partnership between assemblers and tiered networks of suppliers, together with financial institutions and government. Internally there was close collaboration between purchasing, research and development, production, quality, storage and distribution, and marketing. The increasing importance of technological innovation in manufactured products to meet consumer demands more efficiently, combined with the recognition that this was more likely to be obtained from specialist suppliers than from within assembler companies, further enhanced purchasing's position as the means of achieving competitive advantage. Commitment to continuous improvement by driving cost down whilst at the same time improving production processes through supplier development characterizes the best producers.

Whilst the public sector was slower than manufacturing industry to recognize the strategic contribution of purchasing to its objectives, pressures on public expenditure since 1976 have led to a new emphasis on achieving greater economy, efficiency and effectiveness through the Financial Management Initiative. Purchasing's contribution was recognized in the report *Government Purchasing* (Cabinet Office, 1984), followed by the establishment of a Central Unit on Procurement whose annual reports monitor the performance of government departments in respect of savings, organization, training and information systems.

In parallel with these developments, policy on competitive tendering has been progressively implemented in local and central government and the National Health Service, beginning with support services such as cleaning and catering, but extending now to professional areas such as accountancy and legal services.

Recognition of the strategic role of purchasing in government was enhanced considerably by a report on the organization of procurement (Treasury, 1993), which strongly recommended a corporate role for purchasing on departmental top management boards. This is reinforced in the White Paper on government procurement strategy (Treasury, 1995), which values procurement by central government at over £60 billion. Amongst the key elements of the proposed strategy are the following:

- Matching best practice private and public sector organizations in terms of cost savings and value for money.
- Integrated procurement processes covering the whole cycle of acquisition to ensure quality and economy over time.
- Training and skill development to develop world class professional procurement staff.
- Benchmarking to world standards and systematic measurement of effectiveness to support continuous improvement.
- Relationships with suppliers to combine competition with co-operation.

Legislative requirements and concerns about financial accountability and probity which dictate competitive tendering procedures and arms-length relationships with suppliers have traditionally limited the opportunities for purchasing to achieve the value adding benefits demonstrated in the private sector. This may begin to change as a result of the 1995 White Paper. Purchasing also plays a strategic role in meeting wider government social and economic policies, such as sustaining domestic manufacturing capability in key sectors or locations, and assisting small or minority businesses.

Model underlying the purchasing standards

Within the constraints of Standards development outlined in the Introduction to this book, the Purchasing Standards have been drafted in

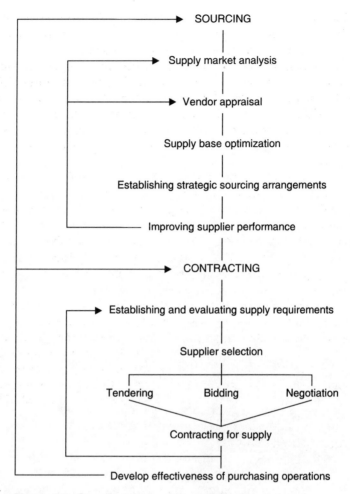

Figure 1.3   Sourcing and contracting model

order to reflect recent theorizations and evidence of a strategic approach to purchasing.

Whilst the core functions of sourcing and contracting are those traditionally identified with purchasing, the Standards seek to encourage an analytical, interactive approach. The model is presented in Figure 1.3. The model assumes that within each sourcing process there may be several or numerous contracting processes. The sourcing process comprises: analysing the supply market; vendor evaluation; optimizing the supply base; establishing strategic sourcing arrangements; and improving supplier performance. Thus sourcing is seen as the process of ensuring that you are buying in markets which are competitive; from suppliers who meet the criteria set by your organization; whose number is neither too large nor too small to meet organizational objectives; with some of which you are seeking to develop closer, longer term relationships to ensure the supply of strategic goods and services;

and to improve their performance. Sourcing may be carried out as a one-off analysis in respect of specific goods or services, or as a general, routine process across all goods and services purchased.

Contracting is then the process of acquiring goods and services from appropriate suppliers identified through the sourcing process. This involves: identifying and specifying requirements and the nature of the supply agreement; selecting the supplier; and negotiating and establishing a contract for supply. Underlying these sourcing and contracting processes is the need to ensure that the performance of the purchasing function is monitored and improved.

Whilst it is argued that this is a logical model which reflects both theory and practice in general, it is not claimed that it is representative of any particular organization, or that every buyer will be involved in all the above tasks in the order set out. In particular, there is clearly a need to establish the organization's requirements, especially those of a strategic nature, to guide the sourcing process. Therefore, as indicated in Figure 1.3, there is a degree of interaction, and iteration, between the sourcing and contracting processes.

Within the contracting process, there are various routes through the supplier selection process: by bids, tenders, or negotiation, or a combination of these methods. All these may be used by the same organization, depending on the nature and strategic significance of the goods and services purchased. Thus, for each contracting process, there may be a different route through supplier selection. Therefore it is expected that a competent purchaser will understand, and be able to carry out, the following tasks, which are covered in the following chapters.

Supply market analysis (Chapter 2)

- Information sources.
- Geographical scope of supply markets.
- Identifying market changes likely to affect supplies: analysing economic trends, national and international legislation, trade agreements, political developments, etc.
- Determining competitiveness of supplies from the market: identifying obstacles to competition; industry structure analysis.
- European Single Market.
- Developing the supply market.

Vendor appraisal (Chapter 3)

- Determine vendor capacity to supply: use of appropriate information sources; criteria for vendor appraisal.
- Evaluating financial viability of supplier: applying financial indices of performance.
- Determining status of potential supplier: importance of good communications with suppliers.

Supply-base optimization (Chapter 4)

- Information sources on suppliers.
- Supply base structures and their implications for optimization.
- Steps in the optimization of the supply base.
- Use of portfolio analysis in analysing the supply base.
- Costs and benefits of rationalization.
- Contracting out as a mechanism for managing the supply base.

Partnership and strategic supply (Chapter 5)

- Characteristics of competitive and partnership approaches to strategic sourcing.
- Advantages of partnership for customer and supplier.
- Applicability of partnership in various sectors.
- Process of implementing strategic partnerships with suppliers.
- Success factors in partnership relationships.

Improving supplier performance (Chapter 6)

- Areas where improvement may be obtained: cost; quality; delivery.
- Methods of monitoring supplier performance through quality standards, vendor rating and quality awards.
- Ways of achieving improvements in supplier performance through close relationships, supplier associations and supplier development.

Establishing and evaluating supply requirements (Chapter 7)

- Planning purchasing requirements.
- Make/do or buy.
- Purpose and methods of specification.
- The process of contracting for services.
- Options for the agreement to supply.

Supplier selection (Chapter 8)

- Identification of potential suppliers: information sources.
- Criteria for selection: quality, quantity, price, etc.
- Methods of selection: bids and tenders – factors affecting which method is to be used.
- Tendering procedures: policy and legal constraints; formal procedures – tender documentation, return of tenders, opening, evaluation.
- Clarification and improvement of offers: resolving queries, clarifying variances from specification, negotiating improvements.
- Communications with successful and unsuccessful bidders.

Contracting for supply (Chapter 9)

- Negotiation of supply agreement.
- Establishing contract for supply: nature of contract; legal aspects; risk; remedies.
- Placing contract: manual and electronic means of transmission; administrative procedures.
- Contractual claims: nature of claim; investigating claims; documentation; resolution.
- Delivery requirements.

Developing effectiveness of purchasing operations (Chapter 10)

- Objectives of purchasing: strategic; departmental; individual; targets and key indicators.
- Improving effectiveness; performance monitoring; evaluation models and techniques.
- World class purchasing: benchmarking; contribution to overall organizational objectives.
- Personality attributes: skills and knowledge characteristic of successful buyers; self-development.

Purchasing's contribution to supply chain strategies

In addition to the above core purchasing functions, purchasing staff may also contribute to wider supply chain strategies, including electronic trading, inventory management, materials management and distribution. The degree of responsibility and involvement of purchasing staff will vary from organization to organization, but developments in these areas will have a significant impact on purchasing's core sourcing and contracting functions. Therefore it is important that you are aware of these developments within your organization, as well having an understanding from suitable sources of general thinking and best practice in these areas.

You will recall from the Introduction to this book that standards for inventory management and materials management, distribution and stores and warehousing have been developed separately from those for purchasing by the Purchasing and Supply and other lead bodies. They do not form part of the core purchasing functions as defined by the Purchasing and Supply Lead Body, and therefore are not covered here.

Electronic trading and electronic data interchange (EDI) underlie many of the purchasing units, and therefore you will be expected to demonstrate knowledge of electronic means of sourcing and contracting. This topic is therefore discussed below.

Electronic trading and EDI

Many organizations are developing integrated purchasing systems to facilitate electronic transfer of documents both within the organization and to suppliers and customers. This requires developing the following components of purchasing systems: requisitioning and ordering; tendering and contracting; EDI; billing and payment; deliveries; stock and inventory control. On behalf of government departments, the Public Competition and Purchasing Unit (1992) has developed a comprehensive specification, with the acronym PURSUIT (purchasing and supply: unified information technology), as a guide to both departments and suppliers as to what is required in an integrated purchasing system. Suppliers are now expected to ensure that their systems are compatible with PURSUIT.

This illustrates the strategic importance of purchasing information systems, in that suppliers may offer their own computer system solution to customers, which can have the effect of locking purchasing in to that supplier. This is a feature of suppliers of drugs and other medical supplies in the USA. Developing your own systems, or establishing the system requirements yourself (as with PURSUIT), means that suppliers must conform to your requirements, which should therefore result in a greater choice of potential suppliers.

EDI is the means by which many organizations now communicate with their suppliers. EDI itself is simply the process of transferring data from the organization's information systems to those of the supplier, rather than using paper-based systems such as mailing.

The following benefits of EDI may be identified:

- Faster data transmission.
- Reduced paperwork.
- Fewer errors in transcription.
- Improved use of transport fleets.
- Lowering of stock levels.
- Better integration between functions.
- May be established as a prerequisite for doing business.
- Quicker access to new, distant markets.
- Improved relationship with suppliers.
- Single input of data, reducing the incidence of errors.
- Better service to customer.
- Faster sale/invoice/payment cycle.

Constraints on the implementation of EDI include:

- Difficulty of identifying suitable partners.
- Technical obstacles, including lack of interconnectivity.
- Absence of message standards.
- Domination by technocrats rather than users.

- Lack of awareness of commercial opportunities by business managers.
- Costs of implementation and difficulty of calculating them.
- Lack of a legal framework to determine status of EDI messages.
- Use of back-up paper copies.
- Difficulty of cost/benefit justification.
- Changes in authorization systems.
- Need for passwords and authentification and audit trails.

Despite these constraints, electronic trading is already an industry standard in the retail sector, with electronic ordering direct from supermarket tills to distribution centres and from there to suppliers, facilitating daily or more frequent deliveries of stock. In manufacturing, computer aided design (CAD) and computer aided manufacturing (CAM) between suppliers and customers are common. The financial services industry uses electronic systems to transfer money between accounts, providing a vast depth of experience in operating electronic billing and payment systems which are increasingly being introduced between customers and suppliers. In addition, as we have seen, the public sector is taking a proactive approach to developing specifications for electronic trading. Thus the strategic importance of electronic trading is bound to increase with its rapid implementation, and you should therefore be aware of its potential for improving purchasing operations themselves, as well as their integration with other functions.

Summary

This chapter has outlined the implications of adopting a supply chain perspective on the role of purchasing. You should as a result be aware of the need to adopt a proactive approach to liaising with other functions in order to achieve the benefits of integrated planning and to extend the scope of your analysis of purchasing activities back down the supply chain to your suppliers and their suppliers. This chapter has also outlined the strategic contribution of purchasing, and you should therefore be able to relate your activities to overall organizational goals and strategies, and see how your work contributes to their achievement. Finally, the model on which the purchasing standards and NVQs and SVQs is based, and which provides the rationale for the content of the chapters which follow, has been outlined. Whilst the chapters are presented sequentially according to logical steps in the sourcing and contracting processes, they may be read separately or in any order, to fit with your progress through the Purchasing Standards or course on which you are engaged. The next chapter will consider the field within which your purchasing activities take place, the supply market and its analysis.

Activities	

1 Write a memo to your Purchasing Manager identifying those aspects of the department's work which are clerical, and those which are strategic, with recommendations for reducing the former and increasing the latter.

2 As part of a staff development programme, your organization is holding a conference which staff from all functional departments, as well as senior management, will attend. You have been asked to present a short paper entitled 'How does purchasing contribute to corporate strategy in our organization?'. List the main points you will make.

References and further reading

Baily, P., Farmer, D., Jessop, D. and Jones, D. (1994) *Purchasing Principles and Management*, 7th edn, Pitman, London

Cabinet Office (1984) *Government Purchasing*, HMSO, London

Carter, J. R. (1993) *Purchasing: Continued Improvement through Integration*, Business One/APICS, Richard D. Irwin, Homewood, IL

Department of Trade and Industry (1991) *Logistics and Supply Chain Management, Management in the 90s*, HMSO, London

Ellram, L. M. and Carr, A. (1994) 'Strategic purchasing: a history and review of the literature', *International Journal of Purchasing and Materials Management*, **Spring**, 10–18

Gadde, L. E. and Hakansson, H. (1993) *Professional Purchasing*, Routledge, London

Gadde, L. E. and Hakansson, H. (1994) 'The changing role of purchasing: reconsidering three strategic issues', *European Journal of Purchasing and Supply Management*, **1**, 27–35

Garnett, P. (1992) *Adding Value Through the Purchasing Function*, CIPS Conference, Solihull, October

Lamming, R. (1993) *Beyond Partnership: Strategies for Innovation and Lean Supply*, Prentice Hall International, Hemel Hempstead

Pearson, J. N. and Gritzmacher, K. J. (1990) 'Integrating purchasing into strategic management', *Long Range Planning*, **23** (3), 91–99

Public Competition and Purchasing Unit (1992) *PURSUIT Operational Requirement: Main Report*, HMSO, London

Syson, R. (1992) *Improving Purchase Performance*, Pitman, London

Treasury (1993) *The Organisation of Purchasing in Government Departments and their Agencies*, HMSO, London, March

Treasury (1995) *Setting New Standards: A Strategy for Government Procurement*, Cm2840, HMSO, London, May

PART TWO

Sourcing

2 Analysing the supply market

Introduction

The external environment is regarded as the most critical variable affecting the performance of organizations. The nature of the environment, whether simple or complex, stable or turbulent, has been found to influence the structure and operations of organizations. The most important environmental aspect for purchasers is the supply market.

The objectives of this chapter are to:

- Identify sources of information for analysing the supply market.
- Examine the geographical scope of the supply market.
- Examine the competitiveness of supply markets.
- Present a model for the analysis of the power of suppliers and buyers in a market.
- Consider the significance of the European Single Market for buyers.

The supply market

Information sources

Basic information about the number and location of potential suppliers, the nature of products, prices charged and forecasts of economic and political stability is an essential requirement if you are to analyse your supply market effectively, rather than simply buy from traditional sources which may not be competitive. You should find the following sources of information useful:

- Company directories and buyers' guides, e.g. *Kelly's Business Directory, Kompass Business Directory, Sell's Products and Services Directory, Thompson Local Directory.*
- On-line databases, e.g. Dun and Bradstreet.
- Current and past supplier records.
- Trade associations (see *Directory of Trade Associations and Professional Bodies of the United Kingdom*, Pergamon Press, Oxford).
- Trade journals for the product or industry.
- Economic and political forecasts for the industry or country, e.g. Economist Intelligence Service.

- Suppliers' representatives.
- Exhibitions and conferences.
- Internal customers.
- The potential suppliers.
- Other buying organizations, especially in the public sector.
- Trading companies and import brokers.
- Subsidiaries.

The following extract illustrates the importance of not relying on published sources alone to gain market knowledge, but to make full use of personal contacts.

Finding out about the supply market

One of the most important activities is market research – knowing where the supply base is going and where our product needs are going, now and in the future. For example, with the move from magnetic to optical discs, the time from evaluation to implementation was about 2 years.

You need to know how to collect information. The most successful ways are reading trade magazines and keeping your eyes and ears open. Talking and listening. Exhibitions are useful for broadening your knowledge of the potential vendor base. Magazine articles are often not very well researched, so you need to listen to the 'industry gossip' and check your information.

Source: Interview, International Buyer, IBM

Geographical scope

Sourcing strategies should include consideration of the markets from which key products and services may be sourced. Whilst for many organizations the local or national market can provide most requirements, in highly competitive industries successful companies operate on a global sourcing basis, although variables such as the nature of the product, how critical it is to organizational effectiveness, and the strengths of local and national markets need to be considered. Reasons for and against local and global sourcing are presented below.

Reasons for buying locally

- Convenience for vendor appraisal and development.
- Delivery and product quality problems are resolved more easily.
- Facilitates just-in-time delivery.

- Assists in developing the local economy.
- Transport costs are low from immediate supplier.
- Rules of origin may require a high percentage of local content (for example, Japanese cars built in the UK must achieve 80% of European Community content to be regarded as EC produced).
- Delivery and response times may be critical.
- Organizational policy, e.g. most public sector organizations have traditionally bought 'national'.

However, if you are buying mainly from local markets, you need to consider whether your supplies are truly competitive. For example, whilst your supplier may be local, the supplies themselves may originate from another country. In this case, you are still paying transport costs, plus your supplier's mark-up.

If you work in the public sector, or for one of the utility companies, you are required by the EC Procurement Directives to invite bids from throughout the Community for contracts above specified thresholds, and not to discriminate against non-national suppliers. This is equally true in respect of the General Agreement on Tariffs and Trade's (GATT) Government Procurement Agreement. The Directives are outlined in Chapter 7.

Whilst the procedures may not necessarily ensure globally competitive supplies, and may overemphasize price, they do force purchasers to test foreign markets. This suggests that, for many buyers, 'local' purchasing is becoming increasingly associated with a much wider geographical area. For a multinational such as IBM, there are good reasons for sourcing the requirements of their European operations from European and national markets.

IBM's European Sourcing Strategy

European Sourcing is an important factor in IBM's purchasing policy. Often, when faced with a Far Eastern supplier, the first imperative is to find a European alternative. The reasons are threefold: shorter lead times and flexibility in the supply chain; the cost of moving currency and satisfying trade and tariff regulations; and IBM's ethical stance on balancing its earnings and spending on a country by country basis.

*Source: Joselyn, L. (1991) 'Procurement task requires a new way of thinking', New Electronics, **January**, 50–52*

Reasons for global sourcing

Despite the constraints such as the legal requirements considered above, there are many positive reasons for sourcing globally:

- Obtaining world class supplies: the best-quality suppliers may not be located locally.
- The product market in which you are buying operates globally, e.g. commodities such as oil.
- The product or technology may not be available locally.
- Exposing the organization to different practices and cultures in order to learn and improve.
- As a means of eventually manufacturing the product locally.
- To achieve the lowest cost supply from a source where wage costs are low and exchange rates are favourable.
- Where countertrade requires a reciprocal import order, i.e. British Airways may agree to buy Boeing on condition that they use Rolls Royce engines.

Clearly, difficulties with transportation, language and cultural barriers, different legal systems, different product standards and specifications, currency fluctuations and political uncertainties are likely to increase with sourcing products globally.

The following extract illustrates the skills and knowledge required in buying commodities on global markets.

Commodity buying in global markets

Buying commodities is different from buying products. With packaging, for example, you need to take an industrial view – what are the production and associated costs, what is the technical ability of the supplier, what is the complexity of what we are asking for? In packaging, the product launch date sets the deadline for purchase timing and volumes. With commodities, the market is governed by supply and demand and sets the price level. You are seeking to buy the right volume of the commodity at an advantageous price. You need to buy at the right time to minimize the cost: not too soon or too late. But commodity markets are different because of their volatility. You need to try and assess what is likely to happen, what affects the price of a commodity. You need to read the 'sentiment' of the market: is it a short term or a sustained movement? You need to make sure that you don't expose the company to unacceptable risk. Political disturbances, such as in the Ivory Coast, can affect prices. You need to build relationships with the processors, get to know them, if you want to be first on their list: they know more about price changes. There are also different prices for different qualities: Ghanaian cocoa is a higher grade than Nigerian or Ivory Coast. Currency is obviously important, especially in an uncertain market: the value of cocoa is a summation of demand from many countries, therefore the relative effects of their currencies against sterling would affect demand.

Source: Interview, Senior Buyer, Nestlé Rowntree

The above interview has added significance in that Rowntree had recently suffered a substantial financial loss through an adverse movement in the price of cocoa (which was not the responsibility of the interviewee!). His opinion was that all you could do is take a view of the market, and do the best you can in a given situation. The following case illustrates the process of buying critical components globally.

Buying components in global markets

Ford differentiate between key and non-key parts in terms of whether they are sourced locally or globally. Thus there is no point shipping low unit cost items such as brackets, but critical and more expensive items such as an injection pump are sourced globally. Prices would be obtained from various suppliers, converted into dollars at current exchange rates, costs of freight, etc. added, to give a delivered price to several plants. Commitments may be made for 3–4 years, but decisions about parts for new models could have implications for up to 15 years, so risk factors would be subjected to sensitivity analysis to test the effect of future changes, for instance, in exchange rates.

Ford do not buy much from Japan as it is very expensive. However there is now a tendency for Japanese parts suppliers to locate in Europe. Thus, just as Bosch are making starter controls in South Wales, Nippondenso have set up a plant to make electronic controls in Portugal.

Source: Interview, Lead Buyer, Ford UK

Although price is clearly not the only or necessarily the most important factor considered, if you wish to source products from markets with a high reputation for quality, such as Germany or Japan, which also have strong currencies, there is always a risk of unfavourable exchange rate fluctuations which make the quality/cost differential too high. Thus there may be a higher risk of having to renege on an agreement to source a product in a foreign market. Suppliers themselves may decide, perhaps with encouragement from major customers (see the Health Service case later in this chapter), to relocate in order to reduce or overcome the cost and risk which otherwise may mean loss of business.

The Ford case also shows the necessity to identify and assess key influences in the supply market and their future direction using forecasting techniques such as trend analysis and scenario planning. The sensitivity of the decision to place an order with a supplier to change in any variables, such as exchange rates, political disorder and industrial unrest, may then be assessed by according weightings to their importance, and estimating the degree of risk in percentage terms.

The discipline of assessing supply markets beyond the customer's own locality, region or country is one that you should employ to ensure that key supplies are actually competitive on a global scale. If you do not ensure the competitiveness of your supply markets, your competitors will certainly do so, to your detriment.

INVESTIGATE

- *What is your own organization's sourcing policy? What products and services are sourced locally, nationally, or globally? What are the reasons for using these supply markets?*

Competitiveness of supply markets

One of the most important aspects in determining whether you are getting a good deal from your suppliers is the economic structure of the supply market. The conditions for competitive markets are that the forces of demand and supply can operate freely. This requires that no individual buyer or seller has such a large share of the market that they can fix the price, and that neither buyers or sellers combine to reach agreements which suppress competition. The following are the main forms of markets where competition is restricted:

- *Monopoly*: where there is one major seller, e.g. telecommunications and the energy sectors in the UK.
- *Oligopoly*: where there are several sellers which combine to dominate the market (see the example on the photocopier market given below).
- *Monopsony*: where there is a single main buyer, e.g. Ministry of Defence for military supplies in the UK.

Measures restricting competition between sellers include:

- Price fixing.

- Sales quotas and restricted outlets.
- Refusal to supply spare parts to third-party suppliers.
- Charging differential prices in different countries, e.g. car manufacturers' price differentials in different EC countries.
- Tying dealerships and distributors to a single source.

These practices may be illegal under national and EC law and, if they are suspected, you should establish the legal position before challenging your supplier. For example, anticompetitive practices have been investigated in the photocopier and shipping markets.

In the case of photocopiers, manufacturers were investigated by the Monopolies and Mergers Commission following claims that they required customers to use toner supplied by them, and refused to supply spare parts and manuals to independent maintenance companies. Although technically the market is competitive, such practices, especially if carried out by several of the major manufacturers, would add to the lifetime costs of using and maintaining the machines, and thereby restrict buyer choice.

The case of shipping again illustrates the importance of the total cost of purchase, especially transport costs, rather than just the product price. It is alleged that under the Transatlantic Agreement, shipowners operating liner services across the Atlantic have established a 'cartel'. The 'shipping cartel' are accused by major British manufacturers, including ICI, United Distillers and Imperial Tobacco, of collusion over price fixing, limiting capacity and extending their influence to road haulage. The latter was a problem also identified by an interviewee from a major local authority buying consortium. Furthermore, the shipping cartel was approved by the European Community, despite complaints from British companies and shippers, indicating that legislation and cases brought under it are subject to lobbying by economic interests, supported by influential politicians and officials.

However, even markets with these concentrated structures may still be competitive if the dominant position arises from the producer's economies of scale, entrepreneurial activities, unique product or technology, or the market is regulated by government to ensure fair prices (as with the utilities in the UK).

The effective geographical scope of the market will also affect the degree of concentration: for example, a monopoly supplier in the UK market may be only one of several oligopolistic suppliers in the EC market and a small player in competitive global markets. The effective scope of competition may however be limited by regional or national barriers to market entry imposing specific standards, duties, customs procedures, testing or import location.

INVESTIGATE

● *Are you aware of any limitations to competition in the markets in which you buy? Are the suppliers engaged in collusive activities which may be illegal? Can you do anything about it in conjunction with other buyers?*

The Office of Fair Trading (OFT) has discovered secret agreements to fix prices or share markets in many areas including the supply of ready-mixed concrete, float glass, fuel oil, gas-fired boilers, thermal insulation, polythene pipes as well as estate agency and travel agency services. The OFT has produced a booklet to assist Purchasing Officers who suspect that they may be the victim of a cartel. Some of its main points are outlined below.

Price fixing and market sharing

Agreements to fix prices can take many forms, including agreements on discounts, credit terms, price differentials or price increases as well as agreements to charge the same price.

Analysis of price movements over time can be useful in detecting price-fixing cartels. In particular, any narrowing of the spread of different firms' prices of a particular product may indicate an agreement among them to restrict competition. Computerized price monitoring systems may assist in detection.

Market sharing cartels involve firms deciding on the market share each is to enjoy, and then determining which firms will get which contracts through bid-rigging or collusive tendering. The main techniques are: bid suppression, by which some firms do not bid or withdraw their bids; complementary bidding, by which some firms price too high or include unacceptable terms; and bid rotation, by which firms take turns at being the lowest and winning bidder.

The booklet sets out a number of questions which Purchasing Officers should ask if they suspect a cartel:

● Does the industry or the product have characteristics which make it easier to organize, police and sustain a cartel, e.g. few sellers, homogeneous products, similar costs of production?

● Are there factors which encourage suppliers to make a cartel agreement at a particular time, for example, the development of widespread excess capacity or recession?

● Do prices change or behave in ways that would not be expected?

- Do price changes over time reveal so regular and systematic a leader/follower situation as to be inexplicable without some kind of contact between suppliers?
- Are similar phrases or explanations used in announcing price changes?
- Are 'give-away' phrases sometimes used in correspondence or conversation, for example, 'The industry has decided that margins must be increased to a more reasonable level'?
- Do suppliers exchange information, for example, on sales, market shares, forecasts or investment plans?
- Do suppliers get together frequently, socially or for business purposes, for example at trade association meetings on statistics or standards?

The OFT encourages Purchasing Officers who suspect a cartel to inform the Director General, as a result of which an investigation may be launched. This may result in the cartel being quickly discontinued, and ultimately reference to the Restrictive Practices Court. If a purchaser finds that it has paid over the odds for goods or services because the supplier is a member of an illicit cartel, it can seek to recover the extra costs, either by taking action in the courts or by settling out of court.

The OFT also recommends that a warranty to the effect that suppliers are not party to a cartel be inserted into contracts, or that liquidated damages clauses could be inserted providing a pre-estimate of the loss to the purchaser should the contract be found to have been influenced by a cartel.

Source: Office of Fair Trading, Cartels: Detection and Remedies: A Guide for Purchasers, *HMSO: London, September 1994*

Industry structure analysis

Industry structure analysis may be used to provide a more detailed examination of the organization's immediate competitive environment.

Porter's (1980) model provides the basis of an analysis of competitive forces in global markets, including the relative strength of buyers and suppliers. He argues that the intensity of competition in a market is determined by five competitive forces:

- The degree of rivalry between industry competitors.
- The bargaining power of suppliers.
- The bargaining power of buyers.
- The threat from potential market entrants.
- The threat from potential substitute products.

Whilst Porter's primary emphasis is on marketing strategies, the model may also be used to assist in the development of purchasing strategies. Thus the power of buyers is strongest when:

- It is concentrated or purchases large volumes relative to seller sales.
- The products it purchases represent a significant fraction of the buyer's costs or purchases.
- The products purchased from the industry are standard or undifferentiated.
- The costs of switching to a different supplier are low.
- It earns low profits.
- Buyers pose a credible threat of backward integration, i.e. taking over the supplier company or making the product themselves.
- The industry's product is unimportant to the quality of the buyer's products or services.
- The buyer has full information.

Using this analysis, it is possible to identify the characteristics of industry sectors, such as low competition due to monopoly or a cartel, where supplier power is greatest. Alternatives for buyers in this situation include sourcing the product from a different geographical location, encouraging new suppliers to enter the market, or finding substitute products. New entrants to the market increase the available supply and may use aggressive price competition to gain market share. However, they may have to overcome the following barriers to entry:

- Economies of scale (of existing suppliers).
- Product differentiation.
- Capital requirements.
- Switching costs.
- Access to distribution channels.
- Cost disadvantages independent of scale.
- Government policy.

Alternatively substitute products or processes may perform the same function, provide better performance or be at a lower price than those currently purchased.

Other strategies which may improve your supply market strength are:

- To make your organization more attractive to suppliers, perhaps by reducing the administrative costs of doing business with you.
- To use generic, functional specifications rather than brand names or detailed designs (see Chapter 7).
- Increase suppliers' switching costs, for example by trading electronically or encouraging suppliers to lease storage space on your premises.

- Increase your volume purchased without increasing your own switching costs.
- Buy in low-cost competitive markets, e.g. Eastern Europe.
- Ensure that suppliers deal with purchasing staff rather than users directly.

However, as the Porter model is based upon the assumption that buyers and suppliers are in an adversarial zero sum game where conflict is inevitable, it does not allow for co-operative, non-zero sum relationships such as partnership (see Chapter 5). If the organization's network of suppliers is regarded as the most effective way of achieving competitive advantage through their technical innovation and product quality, then Porter's analysis would need to be applied to competitive groupings of buyers and suppliers, in which the calculation of relative buyer and supplier power would be redundant. Thus, in the global automobile market, the close relationships between Japanese manufacturers such as Toyota and Nissan and their first-, second- and third-tier suppliers lead to technical innovation, faster new product development, continuous cost reduction and improved product quality. As the manufacturers and their suppliers are also in competition, there is constant pressure to improve performance in order not to lose market share. By contrast, manufacturers in Europe and North America who operated on an adversarial basis have, in line with Porter's analysis, been outperformed by the Japanese and other Pacific rim countries.

INVESTIGATE

- *Analyse the market for a product or service you purchase using the Porter analysis. Is it a buyer or supplier market? If the former, are you making full advantage of your strength? If the latter, can you apply strategies to increase your own strength?*

The European Single Market

Daems (1990) provides a useful example of how the model may be applied to markets in general, showing the prospective threats and opportunities for buyer and supplier companies in the EC Single Market. He assesses the impact of the Single Market on Porter's five competitive forces as follows.

Rivalry

- Disappearance of traditional market boundaries.
- Lower cost production through relocation.
- Greater economies of scale.

- Unused productive capacity.
- Common product specifications leading to new products being offered throughout the EC.

The effect of these changes will be to break down collusive market sharing arrangements in the short term, but mergers and strategic alliances will increase concentration in the longer term.

Buyer power

Buyers will have more options because it will be more difficult for suppliers to sustain price discrimination, as they should be able to buy direct from multinationals' sales offices in any EC country.

Supplier power

Suppliers will be able to deliver goods and services throughout the EC at lower cost, and will be able to relocate more easily so they will not be tied to a single local or national buyer.

Market entry/substitutes

- Costs of transportation, inspection and documentation will be lower so it should be easier to penetrate new markets.
- A single product specification should facilitate access to EC-wide markets as national differences in products and standards are removed.
- Efficiency of product development and innovation should be improved.

What evidence of the changes suggested by Daems does the advertisement shown in Figure 2.1 provide? There is certainly evidence to support reduced transportation time and costs, leading to easier market entry. There is also evidence to support increased supplier power, in that it will be easier for their products to be delivered to markets outside their country of origin, and thereby reduce their dependence on a dominant buyer. The 30% reduction in price may reflect increased competition, either actual or threatened, between transportation companies. This in itself will help to increase buyer power because, with transportation costs falling, domestic suppliers will have to take the threat of foreign suppliers more seriously.

WHEN
EUROPE'S TRADE
BARRIERS
CAME DOWN
SO DID
UPS DELIVERY
TIMES.
(AS WELL AS
MOST OF OUR
RATES.)

After all the anticipation,
UPS is pleased to announce some tangible benefits
of the single European market. Because we can now cross borders
with less fuss and fewer delays, we have been able
to reduce transit times for many of our European ground deliveries.
And we've also reduced our rates by up to 30%.
We've always aimed to offer the most predictable deliveries.
But it's equally predictable, with UPS,
that if we can perform our task more efficiently,
we pass the savings on to you.
In this case, savings in time as well as money.

As sure as taking it there yourself.

Call 0800 456789 for further information.

Figure 2.1 Reduced transport costs. (Reproduced by kind permission of United Parcel Services)

What effects of the Single Market identified by Daems does the following extract illustrate?

Xpelair

Xpelair's Technical Director Tony Hayward is – if you'll excuse the pun – a big fan of the European Single Market.

He feels that harmonization of product standards and testing procedures will help his company overcome many of the serious obstacles traditionally associated with trade across the Channel and open up profitable new markets. Xpelair has been trading with other Member States for some years and Tony Hayward views the harmonization process positively.

Explains Tony: 'Xpelair produces around 90 products – but when we export we have to produce on average two versions of each product to meet the varying specifications demanded by other European countries. In the past there have also been very long delays in testing products in some Member States – all of which has acted as an obstacle in trading across Europe.'

Now that is about to change thanks to the series of 'New Approach' directives, which aim to remove both product and testing barriers – and introduce common standards in every Member State . . .

'The bottom line is that the Single Market will enable us to streamline our production processes, because we have fewer variations to make, and boost our sales by reducing approvals delays in Member States. Basically, this means we can concentrate on servicing the needs of our customers, rather than spending an inordinate amount of time meeting the requirements of the approvals authorities.'

Source: Department of Trade and Industry, 'Fresh approach', Single Market News, **Summer**, *1992, p. 22*

The above extract clearly illustrates the effects of having single product specifications resulting in increased rivalry between suppliers, greater opportunities for lower cost market entry based on existing products, and therefore increased buyer power. You should also note that one of the primary effects of national product specification and testing was to protect national producers. This meant that buying similar products from other European countries was more difficult, and because national producers did not have to compete with suppliers from other countries, prices were higher than they would otherwise have been. Common product specifications, and the acceptance in all EC countries of product tests carried out in any one of them, should result in more competition, and therefore greater buyer power. However, Daems also warns of the likely increase in concentration, and it is feasible that, over time, in some sectors one supplier's product may develop a dominant position.

INVESTIGATE

- *Have you noticed any differences in your supply markets since the completion of the EC Single Market? What are the benefits and the costs for your organization? How can you take advantage of the changes outlined by Daems?*

Developing the supply market

If your analysis of the supply market suggests that you are at a disadvantage in relation to suppliers of a particular product or service, the following case demonstrates that a positive approach to developing the market by attracting new suppliers may be effective.

Health Service precooked frozen food market

The Health Service in Northern Ireland examined the options for the supply of frozen foods for hospital patients. These were to:

1. Buy frozen foods commercially.
2. Buy from a British NHS region which had a cook–freeze unit.
3. Install its own cook–freeze unit.

As there were no available commercial sources, and there was insufficient capital to install its own cook–freeze unit, Option 2 was selected for the short term. However, it was decided to examine the European supply market for precooked frozen meals. Whilst the UK frozen food market is very competitive, they had only recently started to supply the NHS, so it was an advantageous time to encourage market entry.

A survey of French suppliers found the following negative and positive factors.

Negative
The main barriers to entry were seen as:

*   Discriminatory product standards and technical specifications.
*   Legislative differences for health, safety and environmental standards.
*   Few suppliers were aware of the implications of the EC public procurement directives.

Positive
*   Half of the suppliers already exported to Britain using distributors, so there were no logistical obstacles to delivery.
*   Suppliers believed that the elimination of border controls would lead to faster and more efficient delivery and reduced costs.
*   Suppliers believed that there was an untapped export market in the UK.

With the likely reduction in barriers to entry as a result of the Single Market, there were incentives for French suppliers to enter the Northern Ireland market through distributors in Britain, thereby increasing competition for supply and reducing costs for the Health Service in Northern Ireland.

Source: S. McMaster (1993) 'The implications of the effect of the Single European Market on the development of supply sources in Europe for the Northern Ireland Health and Personal Social Services' pre-cooked frozen meals contract', M.Sc. Project, University of Ulster

Summary

This chapter has examined how you may identify information about your supply markets, analyse their structure and the power of suppliers and buyers, and seek positively to develop the market for the benefit of your organization. Whilst the economic theories and analytical models for the examination of competitiveness in supply markets are complex, and experts are by no means in full agreement on their nature and application, it is possible to apply them in a practical setting. This does not necessarily require a lot of resources and massive amounts of information. It does require some research and analytical skills but, above all, a challenging and proactive approach to your dealings with suppliers and the markets in which you buy.

Activities

1

In respect of an important area of purchase for which you are responsible, write a memo to your Purchasing Manager outlining the steps you would take in assessing the competitiveness of your current supply against local, national and global sources. You should identify the advantages and disadvantages of each option, as well as the costs involved in researching the market (e.g. time and travel).

2

Identify an area of supply where the level of competition or choice between suppliers is restricted. How would you set about encouraging new suppliers to enter the market? Are there aspects of your organization which might discourage new entrants from doing business with you, e.g. tendering procedures, inefficient administration, late payment? Write a brief paper identifying the steps to be taken by purchasing and other departments in order to encourage new market entrants.

References and further reading

Birou, L. M. and Fawcett, S. E. (1993) 'International purchasing: benefits, requirements and challenges', *International Journal of Purchasing and Materials Management*, **Spring**, 27–37

Daems, H. (1990) 'The strategic implications of Europe 1992', *Long Range Planning*, **23** (3), 41–48

Hickman, T. K. and Hickman, W. M. (1992) *Global Purchasing: How to Buy Goods and Services in Foreign Markets*, Homewood, Irwin, CA

Hines, P. (1993) 'Integrated materials management: a post-Porterian paradigm?', *Proceedings of the 2nd International Conference of IPSERA*, University of Bath

Lamming, R. (1993) *Beyond Partnership: Strategies for Innovation and Lean Supply*, Prentice Hall, New York

Min, H. and Galle, W. P. (1991) 'International purchasing strategies of multinational US firms', *International Journal of Purchasing and Materials Management*, **Summer**, 41–50

Monczka, R. and Trent, R. J. (1992) 'Worldwide sourcing: assessment and execution', *International Journal of Purchasing and Materials Management*, **Autumn**, 9–19

Porter, M. E. (1980) *Competitive Strategy: Techniques for Analyzing Industries and Competitors*, Free Press, New York

Stevens, J. (1995) 'Global purchasing in the supply chain', *Purchasing and Supply Management*, **January**

3 Vendor appraisal

Introduction

The need to examine potential suppliers through vendor appraisal is recognized in most organizations, though the process may range from systematic examination of every supplier by a specific department to assessment on an exceptional basis by particularly enthusiastic purchasers. The main purpose is to ensure that suppliers with which the organization does business can meet the organization's requirements before supply agreements are concluded, so as to avoid the expensive and time-consuming process of dispensing with a supplier who turns out to be unsatisfactory. This requirement is clearly most important for suppliers with which the organization is seeking long-term relationships.

The objectives of this chapter are therefore to:

- Suggest when to use vendor appraisal.
- Illustrate the process of vendor appraisal.
- Present criteria against which potential suppliers may be evaluated.
- Examine how the financial viability of suppliers may be assessed.

Vendor appraisal is distinguished from vendor rating or evaluation (see Chapter 6) in that, in principle, it is carried out before the supplier under appraisal is awarded any business. *Vendor rating* is then the process of monitoring performance continuously against agreed criteria, and *vendor evaluation* may be a periodic review of the supplier's performance which takes place after the contract to supply has been completed. This is supported by Porter (1991), who distinguishes between process-based evaluation, which is carried out before supply takes place, and performance-based evaluation, which is carried out after supply. This is illustrated in respect of Intel below.

Process and performance evaluation: Intel

'First we do some analysis on all the reasonable players. We look at who participates in the market, we analyse their financial strength, we try to benchmark companies within a particular SIC code where possible. Then we do a quality audit.'

Process-based evaluation addresses longer term supply base management aims. It is usually carried out by a multifunctional audit team, often quality led but including purchasing and engineering staff: 'We try to assess how it does its manufacturing, how it manages quality, how it trains employees, what kind of leadership it has. We're looking for a cultural fit. Does it have the same values?'

Performance-based evaluation relates to short-term tactical purchasing objectives, based on supplier history. 'That's where our ranking and rating system comes in. This is where we look at supplier performance. We allocate business among the suppliers based on points earned. The worst performing suppliers will still get a percentage of the business though. We give them a chance to improve, but if they never improve, they'll be dropped.'

Source: Roger Whittier of Intel, reported in A. Millen Porter (1991) 'Supplier evaluation revisited', reprinted from Purchasing, *24 October, 111 (6), 58–64. Copyright by Cahners Publishing Company.*

However, in practice, vendor appraisal and evaluation may merge, in that all organizations already have a supply base before they introduce a system of vendor appraisal, and it may also be used to assess an existing supplier's capacity or suitability to expand its supply to the organization. Thus appraisal and evaluation are part of a cyclical process by which an organization may seek to assure that its potential suppliers can deliver to the organization's requirements. Assessing your existing supply base may also be part of its optimization, which is discussed in Chapter 4.

Figure 3.1 provides a useful overview of the supplier selection process in DAF Trucks. The process incorporates vendor appraisal, and indicates its central role in sourcing strategy. The main points illustrated by this example are:

- When and with which suppliers appraisal is carried out.
- The importance of assessing both commercial and technical feasibility.
- The outcomes, and the importance of providing those suppliers approved or conditionally approved with advice and assistance to meet the organization's requirements.

INVESTIGATE

- *Does your own organization have a formal process for evaluating potential suppliers? What steps are involved? How does it relate to the process in DAF Trucks?*

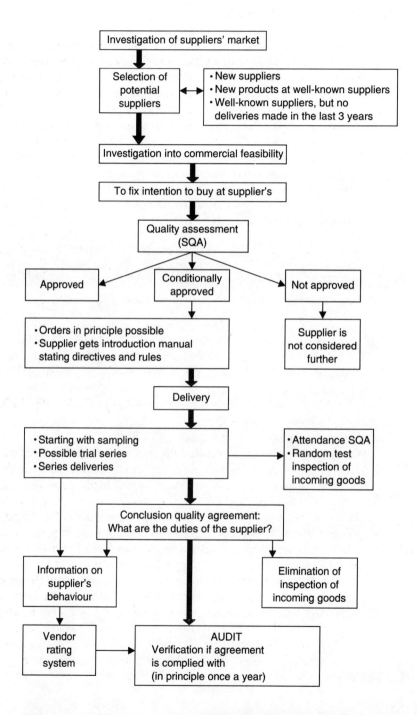

Figure 3.1 Vendor appraisal in DAF Trucks. (From J. Snijder, 'Supply enhancement for the '90s: DAF Trucks', *Institute of Purchasing and Supply National Conference*, London, 15–17 November 1989)

The vendor appraisal process

The identification of potential new suppliers for the goods and services for which the purchaser is responsible should be an ongoing and active, rather than purely reactive, process. You may identify potential suppliers from the sources suggested in Chapter 2. Existing suppliers may also be able to provide additional goods and services to those they already provide. You will first need to inform companies invited to obtain approval as a qualified supplier of the procedures and criteria against which they are to be evaluated. As these may be extremely stringent, involving examination of production processes, quality standards and financial data, it is not a step which either the potential supplier or the purchasing organization should enter into lightly. In particular, you should ensure the confidentiality of data about the potential supplier.

Depending on the relationship between the purchasing organization and the potential supplier, informing them that they will be subjected to stringent evaluation before being allowed to supply may be offputting, if not handled sensitively. Factors in the relationship which will affect the potential supplier's willingness to accept evaluation may include:

- The relative size of purchaser and potential supplier.
- Whether they have done business previously.
- Whether it is a buyer or supplier market for the product (see Chapter 2).
- Whether the potential supplier has supplied other organizations operating a similar system.

Potential benefits for the supplier from undergoing appraisal include not only the obvious one of becoming an approved supplier, but also being able to use its status with a major customer to attract business from other organizations. There will also be the opportunity to participate in supplier development and improvement activities, which are examined in Chapter 6.

Whilst you will probably be able to provide the supplier undergoing appraisal with formal documentation on the nature and operation of the process, it is preferable in addition to arrange meetings with senior managers and staff of the potential supplier to explain the purpose of the process, and in particular that benefits will accrue to both organizations from ensuring that systems and procedures are compatible. Staff from the purchasing organization who will be involved in the process should have the opportunity to meet those with whom they will be dealing in the supplier organization.

Any or all of the following methods of vendor appraisal may be used, in increasing order of interaction with the supplier:

- Checking of references.
- Speaking with previous and current customers.
- Third-party certification, e.g. BS: 5750, Ford Q101.

- Testing of samples.
- Analysis of trading accounts.
- Questionnaires.
- Visits to supplier.
- Audit of supplier.
- Analysis of product costings.
- Analysis of management structures, staffing and administrative procedures.
- Analysis of production and quality processes.
- Analysis of overall financial viability and business performance.

Whilst many of these methods will provide quantitative, objective measures, other qualitative factors are also important, as demonstrated in the Intel case, where overall 'cultural fit' is regarded as important. In other words, is this a company with which you want to develop your business? Do they have the same management philosophies, e.g. on employment of minorities? Do they have compatible production philosophies, e.g. on health and safety and protecting the environment? Are they willing to trade electronically?

Northern Telecom's vendor qualification programme provides a useful illustration of the application of the process.

Northern Telecom's vendor qualification programme

In choosing suppliers, all Northern Telecom purchasing personnel worldwide look at the 'total cost' of ownership, and at the potential for development of long-term relationships with key suppliers, among other factors. Three principles are used to develop the supply base: capability assessments, qualification and certification.

Capability assessments are carried out whenever a new commodity, component family or technology is needed. The assessment determines the potential supplier's ability to service Northern Telecom's current and future requirements, before placing orders for production volumes.

Qualification is the demonstration by a chosen supplier that it is capable of producing a product to Northern Telecom's specifications. The process involves a team survey of the supplier's facility. Qualified suppliers who then show that they have the ability to deliver consistently superior quality products on time may become certified suppliers. And beyond that, a certified supplier who demonstrates leadership in technology, product development and quality may go on a Preferred List. Preferred suppliers receive first consideration for new products or technologies.

The Galway plant was the first in the Northern Telecom group to receive ISO 9000 and they are increasingly looking for suppliers to have it. They also have a growing requirement for EDI (electronic data interchange).

'We have 10 suppliers using EDI at present, and expect to have another 15 by the end of this year, who will account for about 80% of our volume of transactions,' says Mr Bradley (Purchasing Manager). 'I cannot afford to have professional buyers sending out reams of paper any more.'

Environmental considerations are also beginning to loom large, with preference being given to suppliers with an environmental programme in place, and a commitment to eliminate hazardous waste. In January 1992, the Galway plant became the first CFC-free plant in the Northern Telecom group. 'The corporation decided that it would be CFC-free by the end of 1993, but we decided to improve on that deadline,' Noel Bradley comments. 'Now we are looking for our suppliers to be CFC-free in future.'

Source: Extracts from A. Nolan (1994) 'N.T.'s supplier partnership', Professional Purchasing, **April**, *28–34*

Ford Motor Company provides an illustration of the kind of comprehensive vendor appraisal system employed by many major companies, especially in the automotive, computing and aerospace sectors where quality and technical capacity are critical.

Ford's Q101 and supply base management systems

Ford's Q101 system provides a good example of stringent vendor evaluation employed by a major company. Only suppliers' production locations satisfying its requirements are able to supply the company. From a supplier's perspective, the Q101 procedure provides a guide to performance against industry standard ratings, and also a motivating factor to establish internal procedures to ensure performance is improved and maintained. The detailed quality requirements are set out in Box 3.1.

The Q101 system is linked to the overall Supply Base Management process, which assesses quality, technical delivery and commercial aspects of supplier performance in respect of specific products. For each category, suppliers are awarded points against a range of criteria which are weighted to reflect their importance. The criteria are shown in Box 3.2. The outcome for the supplier is to be placed in one of three categories based upon their overall score:

- *Preferred long term*: suppliers achieving the Q101 award and a minimum of 85 in all other categories, who are given sourcing preference over suppliers in the other categories.

Box 3.1 Ford's quality system evidence requirements

Section 3   Achieving process and product quality
3.1   Process capability evaluation
3.2   Use of SPC to monitor processes and improve capability
3.3   Selection of appropriate methods to control all product characteristics
3.4   Adequate gauges, measuring and test equipment for process control
3.5   Conduct and document ES tests as required; react appropriately in case of test failures
3.6   Identification of product and test status
3.7   Written set-up instructions and new set-up verification
3.8   Maintain reference samples
3.9   Procedures for rework operations
3.10 Analysis and documentation of returned parts
3.11 Eight-Discipline reports for quality concerns
3.12 Planning and implementing preventive maintenance
3.13 Control heat-treating operations per Ford standards
3.14 When required, provide lot traceability
3.15 Plans for continuous improvement

Section 2   Planning for quality
2.1   Flow charts of production processes
2.2   Feasibility assessments for proposed new products, changes in processes and products, and major volume changes
2.3   FMEAs for processes and for design when the producer is responsible for the design
2.4   Control plans
2.5   Quality planning for gauging, measuring and testing equipment
2.6   Preliminary process capability studies
2.7   Written process monitoring and control instructions
2.8   Appropriate packaging to protect the product
2.9   Initial sample evaluation, documentation, and certification
2.10 Use data from prototype fabrication in quality planning
2.11 A system to monitor and control subsupplier quality
2.12 Plans for maintaining ongoing quality

Section 4   Documenting quality
4.1   Written quality procedures
4.2   Quality system and performance records
4.3   Drawing and design change control methods
4.4   Part/process modification control
4.5   Process change control methods

Section 5   Special requirements for control item (▽) products
5.1   Use of key quality disciplines for Control Items (▽)
5.2   Documentation for Control Items (▽)

Source: Ford Worldwide Quality System Standard Q-101, *1990, p.4. Reproduced by kind permission of Ford Motor Co. Ltd.*

- *Potential long term*: suppliers who achieve a minimum quality rating of 85 and at least 70 in all other rating categories. These suppliers are judged to have the potential to achieve Preferred Long Term status, normally within one year, and are to be assisted in overcoming any deficiencies identified.
- *Short term*: suppliers who fail to achieve a minimum quality rating of 85 or a minimum score of 70 in any other rating category. This category is used for suppliers who are judged unlikely to achieve a higher status, and who therefore are likely to be eliminated from the supply base.

Box 3.2 *Supply base management criteria*

Commerical
Cost competitiveness
- First year annualized costs
- Ongoing productivity commitment
- Engineering change costs
- Cost savings contribution

Level of support
- Management depth
- Financial resources
- Manufacturing technology/flexibility

Responsiveness to business ideas
- New part launch
- Quotations
- Adaptability
- Responsiveness to buyer and problem-solving situations
- Conformance to Ford tooling and termination claim practices

Supplier delivery rating
- Utilization of Ford Supplier Communication System
- Up-to-schedule shipping performance
- Reaction to problems
- Overshipment
- Record maintenance
- Other supplier performance

Supplier engineering rating
Product design
- Design engineering
- Liaison engineering
- System design
- Component design
- Simultaneous engineering
- Computer-aided design (CAD)
- Computer-aided engineering
- Service engineering
- Programme management

Development
- Development engineering
- Product development
- Material development
- R&D laboratory
- Component prototype build
- Prototype tooling manufacture
- Product launch

Product test
- Test equipment
- Durability testing
- Engineering specification
- Product development testing
- Material

Quality criteria are set out in Box 3.1.

Source: The Supply Base Management Process, *European Automative Operations, January 1991.*
Reproduced by kind permission of Ford Motor Co. Ltd

Ford's Total Quality Excellence (TQE) award is given only to suppliers who achieve a rating of over 90% in all four areas. TQE applies only to suppliers providing full service engineering support and approved suppliers are given preference in business relationship and sourcing decisions. Any supplier rating awarded in the UK is accepted in the USA, and vice versa, so a larger market could open up for suppliers with a high rating.

Sources: Ford Worldwide Quality System Standard Q101 *(1990)*; Ford European Automotive Operations, The Supply Base Management Process, *January 1991; interviews.*

Such large-scale systems are clearly expensive to develop and maintain, but smaller organizations can carry out simpler evaluations without incurring vastly increased costs. A good example is that of a small American computer components supplier, Tricon Industries.

Tricon Industries

Tom Haring, Purchasing Manager, adapted a system used by Motorola, to which Tricon is a supplier. He conducted a cost assessment of Tricon's 125 suppliers through interviews, and set up a manual rating system which resulted in substantial improvements in delivery and quality. On-time delivery improved from 82.6% to 95% in 2 years, quality conformance from 71% to 91%. The benefits, according to Haring, are:

- A more accurate cost of doing business is defined.
- The supplier becomes more aware of buyers' needs and priorities.
- Purchasing from a higher priced supplier can be justified to management.
- Areas of non-conformance are readily seen so immediate action can be taken.
- Suppliers are motivated to improve performance.
- Lower priced suppliers improve performance, realizing that higher priced suppliers are now competitive.
- Higher priced suppliers are grateful for the opportunity to become competitive.

Source: adapted from A. Millen Porter (1991) 'Supplier evaluation revisited', reprinted from Purchasing, *24 October, 111 (6), 58–64. Copyright by Cahners Publishing Company*

Thus the principles and methodology of vendor evaluation may be applied by all purchasing managers, regardless of the size of the organization.

INVESTIGATE

- *Select a major supplier and apply the Ford Supply Base Management system to them. Which of the categories are easy to apply, and which are difficult, perhaps because of the lack of information? Does the overall rating reflect your own impressions regarding the effectiveness of the relationship? How useful therefore do you think the system is as a means of assessing potential suppliers? Can you adapt it to your own organization's needs?*

Vendor prequalification in the public sector

In the public sector it has been common practice to advertise to invite interested suppliers to prequalify for eligibility to tender and, if successful, to be placed on a select list. In the absence of rigorous vendor appraisal, which traditionally has not been carried out in the public sector, select lists may easily become the vehicle for giving business to favoured companies and excluding others equally or better qualified. Whether this is because of lack of purchasing skills, lack of initiative or, in the worst case, fraud, it amounts to poor purchasing practice, which inevitably increases the cost of the purchase.

However, select lists are not permitted for public sector organizations under the EC Directives on Public Procurement, although they are allowed in the form of qualified lists under the Utilities Directive (see Chapter 8 for an outline of the Directives). Prequalification is, however, permitted for each separate contract 'on the basis of information given as to the supplier's personal position and in response to the prescribed questions that may be asked to ascertain if the supplier fulfills the minimum conditions as to eligibility and financial and technical criteria' (Boyle, 1994, p. 106). This is particularly appropriate when the restricted or negotiated procedures are used, in order to ensure an objective and transparent mechanism for selecting the suppliers to be invited to bid. However, as Boyle argues, the prescribed procedures could still result in many suppliers being eligible to participate, and there is no clear guidance on how a manageable short-list of suppliers may be drawn up.

Such prequalification is by no means as rigorous as the vendor appraisal systems outlined above, with the result that public sector organizations are restricted in the extent to which and manner in which they are permitted to refuse to do business with potential suppliers. This does not of course mean that they are forced to select suppliers which they know to be unsatisfactory (perhaps from contracts which the supplier has had with other public sector organizations), but that they may have difficulty in obtaining sufficient information about the potential suppliers in advance of the formal tender. Thus the risk of contracts being awarded to unsatisfactory suppliers is higher in the public sector because rigorous vendor appraisal is not possible prior to tendering, and the number of responses to a tender may preclude extensive appraisal of every respondent.

Financial viability of supplier

Analysis of financial viability is particularly sensitive, but increasingly important if the supplier is likely to become a long-term partner or to supply critical goods or services. You may obtain recent and current details of the company's financial structure and position either directly or from third-party sources, including Companies House or private financial information services. You should try to obtain information on the following:

- Current assets, e.g. capital equipment, cash, debtors.
- Current liabilities, e.g. creditors, bank loans, interest payments.
- Sales volume and value.
- Profits before interest and tax.
- Number and cost of employees.

Analysis of these data is usually carried out by a separate department, though purchasers could usefully seek to develop financial analysis skills themselves so as to have greater control over the process of supplier appraisal and monitoring. The following financial indices of performance may be established from the above data:

- Profit margin: profit before interest and tax divided by sales.
- Annual turnover of capital: sales divided by capital employed.
- Return on capital: profit before interest and tax divided by capital employed.
- Liquidity ratio: current assets divided by current liabilities.
- Sales per employee.
- Profit per employee.
- Debt ratio: debts divided by average sales.

Such ratios provide an indication of the risks likely to be involved in doing business with the supplier, and enable you to compare the financial strength of a number of potential suppliers before selecting those with which you wish to do business.

Status of supplier

As we have seen with the case of Ford's Supply Base Management programme, the result of vendor appraisal is a decision as to the status of the potential supplier, usually as approved, conditional approval or unacceptable. You should communicate the results to the supplier, who may be encouraged to improve those aspects where weaknesses were identified, perhaps through participation in a supplier development programme (see Chapter 6). A detailed record of the supplier's capacity to supply to the required standard against vendor evaluation criteria should be maintained, and you will need to review decisions on the status of potential suppliers at appropriate intervals.

Informing potential suppliers of ratings which are less than satisfactory is clearly sensitive and needs to be handled carefully, as you may wish or need to do business with them in the future. Those conditionally or not approved should be informed of the areas in which they need to improve, and the decision justified with reference to the selection criteria.

Conditionally approved suppliers should be offered assistance to bring them up to the required standard, and periodic review intervals agreed. Even approved suppliers will have areas where improvement will be necessary, and these should be identified and measures for improvement agreed.

Summary

This chapter has illustrated methods of and criteria for vendor appraisal, with reference to a number of cases, the most comprehensive of which is Ford's Supply Base Management system. However, it has also shown that vendor appraisal may be carried out on a much smaller scale by an individual purchasing manager, with benefits to both customer and supplier. As a result you should therefore be more aware of how and under what circumstances your organization appraises its potential suppliers, if at all, and be able to suggest how appraisal may be improved in the light of the cases presented. Techniques of appraisal have also been identified, which may be applied in any organization to assess a supplier's technical and financial capacity to supply, and are a valuable addition to any purchaser's skills. In Chapter 4 we will move on from appraisal to its logical consequence, a slimmer, fitter supply base of qualified suppliers.

Activities

1   Write a brief paper to the Purchasing Manager outlining the strengths and weaknesses of the vendor appraisal process in your own organization, with proposals on how it may be improved.

2   Select a supplier with which you are considering doing business. Outline the steps you would take to obtain information on the supplier's financial viability. Draft a letter stating your intentions and requesting relevant information. Assuming that a face-to-face meeting will be necessary, set out the questions you need to ask. How will you respond should you be asked to provide similar information in respect of your own organization?

References and further reading

Boyle, R. (1994) 'EC Public Procurement Rules – a purchaser reflects on the need for simplification', *Public Procurement Law Review*, **3**, 101–113

Briggs, P. (1994) 'Vendor assessment for partners in supply', *European Journal of Purchasing and Supply Management*, **1** (1), 49–59

Department of Trade and Industry (1993) *Getting the Best from your Suppliers, Managing in the 90s*, HMSO, London

Giunipero, L. C. and Brewer, D. J. (1993) 'Performance based evaluation systems under total quality management', *International Journal of Purchasing and Materials Management*, **Winter**, 35–41

Millen Porter, A. M. (1991) 'Supplier evaluation revisited', *Purchasing*, **111**(6), 58–68

Raia, E. (1990) Medal of Professional Excellence: Ford, *Purchasing*, September, **27**, 41–55

4 Supply base optimization

Introduction

Organizations which purchase from large numbers of suppliers are incurring unnecessary costs, both administrative, and in terms of missed opportunities to standardize the products purchased. A system of vendor appraisal (see Chapter 3) may be used to identify those approved suppliers with which the organization intends to concentrate the majority of its supplies. Those failing to meet the organization's standards may be discarded, thus reducing the range of suppliers with which the purchaser, as well as other administrative departments, has to deal.

The objectives of this chapter therefore are to:

- Establish the strategic importance of the supply base.
- Identify various supply base structures and their implications for optimization.
- Identify information sources on suppliers.
- Outline steps in the optimization of the supply base.
- Demonstrate the use of portfolio analysis in analysing the supply base.
- Examine the costs and benefits of rationalization.
- Explore the use of contracting out as a mechanism for managing the supply base.

Strategic significance of the supply base

The extent of rationalization is likely to be a strategic decision establishing an overall target number of suppliers to be achieved within a set time period, which may then be broken down by product or service area by purchasing managers, so that for each area an optimum number of suppliers is achieved and maintained. Criteria for determining those suppliers to be removed and retained are also likely to be set at senior management level.

Optimization carries with it the implication of extending the supply base to new suppliers for certain products or services, so as not to close off the opportunity to benefit from new technologies or more efficient emerging suppliers. Thus, whilst optimization is likely to result in a smaller number of suppliers overall, those retained may be supplemented by the addition of suppliers new to the organization.

Substantial reductions in the number and range of suppliers have been achieved in recent years by many major companies as part of overall strategies aimed at improving performance. For example, Rank Xerox reduced from 3000 to 500 suppliers by a strategy of centralized supplier base management, worldwide contract volumes, single sourcing and long-term co-operative business relationships with suppliers (Department of Trade and Industry, 1989). The HD Plastics case shows that smaller companies can achieve the benefits of optimizing the supply base equally well.

HD Plastics

This is a company making plastic bin liners, which sought to reduce the number of suppliers of 'masterbatch' colours for the plastics used in the bags. A questionnaire was sent out to the five current suppliers asking for information on their finances, products, personnel, equipment, manufacturing facilities, accreditation, quality systems and customers. Visits were made to the two most suitable firms, one making colours, the other black, white and grey. Between them, these companies provided the full range of colours required, and the two companies were selected. Savings were generated in administration, fewer deliveries and traceability in the case of defects. The two suppliers now have more business, and are prepared to design colour mixes just for HD Plastics. However, the company is continuing to investigate potential new suppliers, although their claims to supply at a cheaper price may hide higher scrap rates, delivery costs or the need to use more colour to achieve the desired quality.

Source: Department of Trade and Industry, Boardroom Report: Best Practice in Purchasing, *Findlay Publications, Horton Kirby, pp.14-17, 1993*

Rank Xerox and HD Plastics show that reduction of the supply base has resulted in improved supplier performance, closer relationships and more business being placed with the remaining suppliers. This chapter is therefore closely related to the strategic issues of partnership sourcing and improving supplier performance examined in Chapters 5 and 6, respectively.

The structure of supply bases

The nature of the supply base varies between sectors and organizations, and, even within organizations, between different products or services. Mapping and understanding the supply base for which you are responsible is the essential first step to its analysis. The following range of supply base structures can be identified.

Unstructured

This may be by neglect or by policy, with any supplier providing the right product at the right price at any time awarded the contract. Any supplier requesting tender documentation or submitting a tender may be added to the supply base, whether awarded a contract or not; and there may be a requirement to add any supplier requesting to be considered for a supply contract so as not to discriminate, especially in the public sector.

Select lists

As we saw in Chapter 3, the overall supply base may be structured for specific product or service areas by select or qualified lists of approved suppliers, though for public sector organizations they may not be compatible with the EC Procurement Directives.

Horizontal networks

Small companies, often family run, pooling expertise or combining to purchase expert professional services, e.g. marketing, computing and legal. There are regular contacts between participants, who are often relatives or personal friends. This structure has been found to be characteristic of the ceramics industry in Northern Italy, light engineering around Lyons in France, and areas such as Northern Ireland with many small and medium size companies, for which the core activity is craft or service based (Johnson and Lawrence, 1988).

US/European manufacturing

Traditionally, there are large numbers of suppliers of parts for assembly on the production line. There will be some subcontracting, but little or no involvement with subcontractors' suppliers. Such supply bases are increasingly being structured by vendor appraisal, as shown by the Ford Supply Base Management system presented in Chapter 3.

Japanese partnership/network sourcing model

Suppliers are structured in up to three tiers. There are a relatively small number (2–300) of first-tier suppliers supplying finished modules, e.g. seat assemblies. Each first-tier supplier may have 25–30 suppliers, who each have a further supply base of 6–10 suppliers. The manufacturer actively manages first-tier suppliers, with partnership relationships and supplier development activities, and expects them to manage second- and third-tier suppliers. The network is bound together by shared financial and ownership relationships, and supplier associations (Hines, 1994).

Lean supply

Similar to Japanese structure, but with more equal relationships between the manufacturer and first-tier suppliers, with the supply base acting as a coherent entity to innovate, add value and reduce waste throughout the supply chain (Lamming, 1993).

Each structure has different implications for optimization. A totally unstructured supply base will need to undergo the 'clean-up' process outlined below. For some organizations, especially in the public sector, legal and policy requirements on ensuring open access and non-discrimination mean that reducing the supply base of active suppliers may not be possible or desirable, but certainly efforts should be made through prequalification to ensure that all suppliers meet the minimum specified criteria. The supply base may also be structured in line with organizational policies on adding any suppliers which are local or small, or from minority or disadvantaged groups.

The strength of horizontal networks lies in the availability of skills and expertise of a large number of small, local firms and agencies, and apart from the obvious need to ensure that the basics of quality, delivery, price, etc., are met satisfactorily, optimization implies working together more effectively, rather than reducing the numbers of suppliers.

In highly competitive manufacturing sectors such as electronics, automobiles, aerospace, etc., optimization is increasingly seen as a means of moving towards partnership or lean supply, with a smaller number of more technically proficient suppliers. For many companies, moving from the traditional manufacturing to a leaner supply base is critical to their survival. Table 4.1 compares Japanese, North American and European motor manufacturers' supply bases, and Figure 4.1 presents the results of efforts by the latter to reduce their supply bases. Figure 4.2 presents Rover's reduced supply base, restructured into tiers as a result of its collaboration with Honda. Methods by which such reductions may be achieved are examined below. However, you should recall that reducing the numbers of suppliers is not an end in itself: optimization also implies the use of systematic vendor appraisal, and possibly developing partnership and supplier improvement programmes so as to ensure that the overall supply base provides the level of performance required.

Information sources on suppliers

In the most highly developed supply base structures discussed above, there is a vendor database which holds details of all suppliers with which the organization is currently doing business, has recently done business, or may be considering for future business. This will be linked to the kind of

Table 4.1
Comparison of Japanese, North American and European automobile manufacturers' supply bases*

Assembler	No. of direct suppliers (domestic supply)	Vehicles built (domestic production; includes commercial vehicles)
Japan		
Toyota	340	3 968 697
Nissan	310	2 213 506
Honda	310	1 293 416
USA/Canada		
GM	2500	5 876 013
Ford	1800	3 982 209
Chrysler	2000	2 207 104
Europe		
Fiat	900	1 880 856
Renault	1050	1 680 636
PSA	900	2 017 508
VW/Audi	1580	1 879 748
D Benz	1650	698 600
BMW	1420	442 776
Porsche	600	25 969
Rover	850	520 299
Jaguar	540	51 939
Volvo	590	331 218
Saab	485	152 406

*All figures apply to 1988, except for BMW, which is 1987.
Source: R. Lamming, *Beyond Partnership: Strategies for Innovation and Lean Supply*, Prentice-Hall International, Hemel Hempstead, p. 172, 1993.

sophisticated vendor appraisal and monitoring examined in Chapters 3 and 6. However, many organizations are far from this ideal. They may have some of the following characteristics:

- Manual records of suppliers, perhaps only in the form of orders or payments.
- Several different computerized systems, for example, purchasing, stores and accounts, which may not be compatible, and contain substantial differences in information.
- Different sets of supplier records in different purchasing departments making an overall organizational perspective difficult to achieve.

If you are in such an organization, you will clearly require considerable research skills first to identify and then to assimilate these various sources.

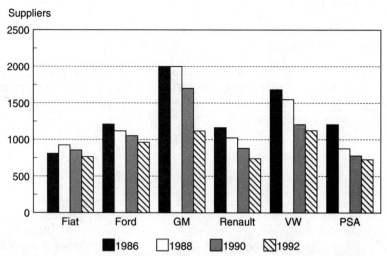

Figure 4.1 An example of strategic reductions in supply bases: European volume assemblers. (From R. Lamming, *Beyond Partnership: Strategies for Innovation and Lean Supply*, Prentice Hall International, Hemel Hempstead, 1993, p. 1)

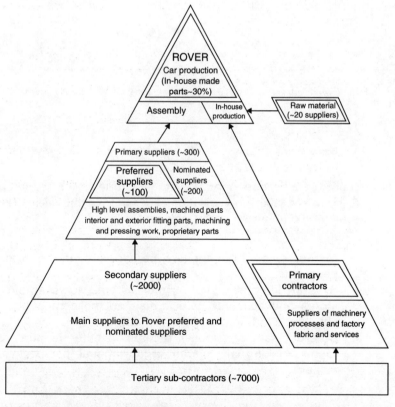

Figure 4.2 Rover's network of suppliers. (From R. Bertodo, 'The role of suppliers in implementing a strategic vision', *Long Range Planning*, **24**, (3), 40–46. Copyright (1991) with kind permission from Elsevier Science Ltd, The Boulevard, Langford Lane, Kidlington OX5 1GB, UK

INVESTIGATE

- *Does your organization have plans which incorporate supply base optimization? What is the nature of your supply base in terms of the structures examined above, and the quality of information sources? How easily can you identify the suppliers with whom your section, department and organization deals?*

Steps in the optimization of the supply base

The starting point is the examination of existing suppliers in relation to the value of business conducted. This may be done using Pareto analysis. Thus organizations which have not recently analysed their supply base will probably find that roughly 80% of supplies by value may be supplied by 20% or less of their suppliers. Clearly, therefore, the long tail of low-value suppliers is the target for rationalization, subject to how critical the product or service purchased is.

A series of practical steps towards rationalization is provided by Basu (1993). These are as follows:

- *General clean up*: remove from the list of vendors:
  - Those which have ceased operating
  - Those which have changed name due to change of ownership
  - Those whose name may have been entered twice differently
  - Those who have different trading, distribution or invoice addresses.
- *Frequency of use*: identify vendors with only one, then two, one-off orders over a 2-year period.
- *Functional categorization*: examine suppliers to only one department, e.g. production, research and development, to see if there is a continuing need for them.
- *Commodity-based rationalization*: in each commodity area identify a number of sources and rationalize, taking risk elements, such as the security of supply, into consideration.
- *Single sourcing*: many non-critical items (see Purchasing Portfolio Analysis below), such as standard raw materials, fasteners, office stationery, etc., are freely available and purchases could be concentrated in a single supplier with economies-of-scale benefits and very low risk.
- *Subcontract*: products currently manufactured in-house for which there is a specialist supplier may be subcontracted, thus transferring the management of the vendor base to a subcontractor (see Contracting Out, below). Basu gives the example of printed circuit boards, for which, instead of dealing with many separate suppliers

for artwork, printed circuit blanks, printing and electronic components, a specialist subcontractor supplies complete boards.

Basu suggests that a general clean-up and frequency-based reduction should be conducted every 6 months, whilst the other aspects should be subject to annual review.

Purchasing portfolio analysis

Kraljic (1983) presents an approach to analysing strategic purchasing options using portfolio analysis. This takes into account the relative strengths of buyer and supplier, and assesses risks such as the effect of selected strategies on security of supply. The starting point is the categorization of purchases into four groups, which are set out below with their implications for the supply base:

Non-critical purchases

These are usually low-value, high-volume items with a wide choice of suppliers. Thus there are opportunities for standardization of products, reduction of inventory and concentration of business in a smaller number of suppliers. Purchase of such products may also be itself contracted out to another company or agency, thus transferring the administrative costs from the core organization.

Bottleneck purchases

These may be low-value products, but are not easily obtainable. They therefore carry a high risk of supply failure, and stronger links with suppliers of such products, as well as alternative suppliers, should be developed.

Leverage purchases

There are many suppliers of products but few buyers for these items, and therefore the buyers may profit from competitive bidding procedures with suppliers without the need to develop stronger or longer term relationships.

Strategic purchases

These items are scarce, high value, with few suppliers and there is limited competition from new market entrants. For such items longer term relationships with existing suppliers should be developed.

Thus the main focus for rationalization should be suppliers of non-critical and leverage items, with suppliers of bottleneck and strategic items targeted for possible partnership.

Rationalization of the supply base in the automobile industry

Lamming (1993, pp. 181–183) identifies the following ways by which motor manufacturers have sought to reduce their supply base:

- Removal of any supplier who does not meet required levels of performance in Supplier Quality Assurance and other supplier assessment processes.
- Moving from several sources to dual or single sourcing.
- Integration of several separate components into a redesigned, possibly less complex subassembly which is assembled by a direct or first-tier supplier; suppliers of smaller components switch supply to the subassembler.
- Use of first-tier suppliers to co-ordinate supply from minor firms, i.e. outsourcing assembly work to specialist companies, often paying lower labour rates (e.g. cutting and sewing of fabrics and leather); thus seating systems are supplied whole by one supplier, rather than having 30 suppliers of 50 pieces delivering to the manufacturer's assembly line.

The rationale for the adoption of the methods outlined above, and evidence of the enhanced role of suppliers is provided by the case of Volkswagen presented below.

Volkswagen's supply base policy

Volkswagen's goal is to source the entire purchasing volume from 'best in world' suppliers, offering the 'highest quality at the lowest price, at the right place and at the right time'. Extensive sourcing programmes are already under way in the UK, France, Spain and Italy involving contact with 390 suppliers.

The challenge facing the motor car industry today is principally pressure of costs. This is due, amongst other things, to higher development costs resulting from more frequent model changes and technically more sophisticated vehicles, new safety features, and higher overheads from increased advertising and marketing expenditure. This has resulted in a requirement for constant adaptation, including changes in purchasing policy in an attempt to make offsetting reductions in costs. This has led in turn to international production locations, improvements in quality, higher requirement profiles for the developers of component parts and a stricter adherence to deadlines.

Other changes include the reduction of material costs and an increase in the proportion of recyclable parts in order to meet future environmental requirements now.

The classic supplier relationship is increasingly being supplanted by more complex forms of co-operation. Part of the development and quality responsibility is transferred to the supplier, who also takes over certain logistical functions. For example, highly automated vehicle assembly requires the supply of complete subassemblies. In future, Volkswagen's suppliers will more frequently have 'module' responsibility for an assembly comprising very different types of component, e.g. painted bumpers with fog lamps, a steering wheel with an air bag, or a complete seat with an integrated safety belt.

In this context, Volkswagen see the possibility of module suppliers themselves procuring parts for the module from low-cost sources. Final assembly might then take place in a satellite factory in the vicinity of the vehicle assembly plant.

Volkswagen's criterion for the sourcing decision is the best compromise of price, logistical optimization, technical and quality levels, and, where appropriate, considerations relevant to the sales market. The supplier industry has a central function in this procurement strategy, filling the role of problem solver, making use of all its potential for innovation, structural adaptation and international mobility.

*Source: Department of Trade and Industry, 'Opportunities for suppliers', Single Market News, **Autumn**, 9, 1992*

INVESTIGATE

- *Can you apply the steps towards rationalization outlined above to your own supply base? How would you categorize your suppliers using purchasing portfolio analysis? Are the methods of rationalization outlined by Lamming appropriate to your organization and its supply base? Are your suppliers delivering the innovation required by Volkswagen?*

Contracting out

A significant strategic option for managing the supply base is that of the contracting out of support activities, so that the organization can concentrate on its core activity (see Chapter 5). As well as the benefits of cost reduction

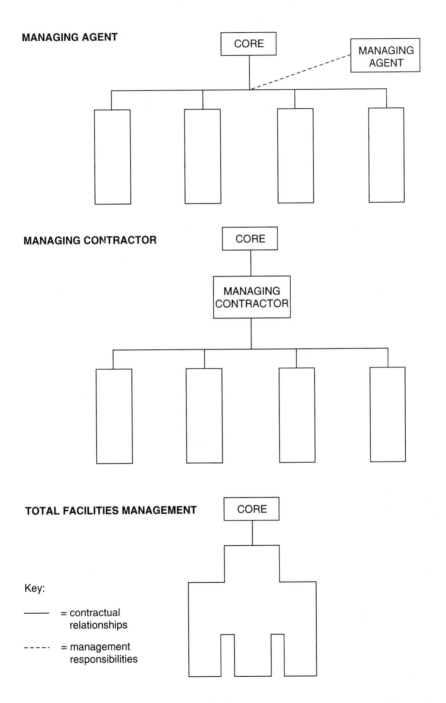

Figure 4.3 Options for managing service and works contracts. (Reproduced with kind permission of Symonds Facilities Management Inc.)

and improved performance which normally ensue, the need to purchase supplies to maintain such operations may be removed. The effects of contracting out on the supply base will, however, vary depending upon how the contractors are to be managed. Should the client organization decide to manage all service contracts themselves, the client managers let contracts for non-core services directly, and are responsible for managing and monitoring the contracts. This results in a substantially increased workload for purchasing or line managers and an increased number of suppliers for work previously carried out in-house.

The following alternatives for simplifying the management of works and service contracts may be identified (see Figure 4.3).

Managing agent

The client enters into separate contracts with the managing agent, works contractors and support consultants. All administration and procurement is undertaken by the managing agent on behalf of the client. However, the client still has a direct contractual relationship with all the service contractors; the benefit comes from the expertise of the managing agent in selecting and managing the contractors.

Managing contractor

In this scenario, the managing contractor sets up contracts for support services directly with a range of service providers. The client organization has no direct contractual relationship with the service contractors, thus the number of suppliers to be managed directly is reduced, and there is only one point of contact, with the managing contractor. However, this carries greater risks for the client organization, in that it is dependent upon the managing contractor to protect its interests, rather than to collude with the service suppliers for their mutual benefit. There is also a loss of technical expertise in managing service contractors. In terms of supply base structures, this model is similar to the outsourcing of subassemblies in manufacturing discussed above.

Total facilities management

This is similar to the previous model, but the facilities management company provides all services either directly or by contracting with other service suppliers. Service suppliers may be a combination of in-house and contracted out. This has a similar effect on the supply base as the previous model, and in both cases there is a need to have very effective control mechanisms in the contract to protect the client.

You should therefore be aware of the benefits and risks of the above options, and especially the effects of having a single contract for all services, with resultant benefits in terms of a reduced direct supply base, or multiple contracts with benefits in terms of control and flexibility, but greater responsibility for managing and monitoring contractors' performance.

INVESTIGATE

- *Does your organization contract out its works or services? Which of the above models are used, and what are the effects in terms of managing the supply base?*

Costs and benefits of rationalization

You should consider the costs and benefits of rationalization before proceeding to prune your supply base radically. The costs may include:

- Sunk costs of investment in current suppliers who are not kept on; however, as these cannot be recovered, they should be discounted.
- Costs of disposing of current suppliers with which contracts are still in place.
- Loss of expertise in technology or service performance.
- The acquisition costs of building and maintaining relationships with new suppliers such as the time necessary to adjust to new products, processes and organizational cultures, as well as additional visits, meetings and the alignment of systems.
- Increased risks to security and competitiveness of supply.

However, the long-term benefits of trading with fewer, expert suppliers are likely to far outweigh the short-term costs of discarding unsatisfactory suppliers. Benefits include:

- Less time spent in remedying defects or poor performance, and on contractual disputes.
- Fewer supplier files need to be maintained, e.g. vendor rating, correspondence, delivery schedules, orders, accounts, resulting in financial, storage and time savings.
- Access to the expertise of specialist companies.
- More time to devote to developing and improving relationships with remaining suppliers, leading to better performance of products and services, administrative processes, delivery, etc.

The benefits outlined above are clearly demonstrated in the case of Glaxo.

Supplier reduction in Glaxo

As part of an overall strategy aimed at improving the value added by purchasing, Glaxo's supply base of over 4500 live suppliers, including 27 suppliers of stationery, was examined. The resource consequences of this large number of suppliers and the high volume of orders lay in the amount of staff time taken up with matching orders, invoices and goods received notes, and rejecting and following up mismatches. Through a policy of software development, umbrella contracting, single sourcing policy, order collation and changes in attitude, the incidence of low-value order processing was reduced significantly. Single sourcing became prevalent, with requisitioners able to communicate directly with suppliers within an umbrella contract. The key supplier base was reduced to 30 for over 80% of group spend and 10 suppliers receive over 60%. Considerable integration has also been achieved between these suppliers, Glaxo and their suppliers.

Source: P. Garnett, 'Adding value through the purchasing function', CIPS National Conference, Solihull, October 1992

Thus, the professional expertise of the purchaser is critical in order for the benefits from rationalization to outweigh the costs, i.e. for the supply base to be optimized, and to ensure that the organization is adequately protected against increased risks.

INVESTIGATE

- *What are the main costs and benefits of reducing your own organization's supply base? How can you demonstrate added value through optimizing the supply base?*

Summary

This chapter has outlined the importance of active management of the supply base in order to ensure that it is optimal for the organization. This means achieving the right balance between benefits from a reduced number of suppliers with the required expertise, and increased risks to security, competitiveness of supply and loss of direct control over non-first-tier suppliers or contractors. It has also been emphasized that the optimal balance may vary between product and service areas, depending on their value and the degree to which they are critical. You should therefore be able to analyse the supply base for the products and services for which you are responsible using the methods outlined above, and demonstrate how a proactive approach can bring benefits to your organization.

Activities

1 Using the methods suggested by Basu, Kraljic and Lamming, carry out an analysis of the suppliers for which you are responsible to determine whether and to what extent your supply base may be reduced.

2 The Purchasing Manager has asked you for ideas which he or she can use in a paper on reducing costs and improving performance through better management of the supply base. The paper is to be presented at a Board Meeting attended by heads of marketing, production, finance and other departments. List the points you would suggest, emphasizing the benefits and risks for the organization as a whole from optimizing the supply base.

References and further reading

Basu, S. K. (1993) 'Vendor base reduction', *Purchasing and Supply Management*, **June**, 32–33

Bertodo, R. (1991) 'The role of suppliers in implementing a strategic vision', *Sloan Management Review*, **Spring**, 40–48

Department of Trade and Industry (1989) *Partnership Sourcing*, HMSO, London

Department of Trade and Industry (1993) *Boardroom Report: Best Practice in Purchasing*, Findlay Publications, Horton Kirby

Garnett, P. (1992) 'Adding value through the purchasing function', *CIPS National Conference*, Solihull, October

Hines, P. (1994) *Creating World Class Suppliers: Unlocking Mutual Competitive Advantage*, Financial Times/Pitman, London

Johnson, R. and Lawrence, P. R. (1988) 'Beyond vertical integration – the rise of the value-adding partnership', *Harvard Business Review*, **Jul–Aug**, 94–101

Kraljic, P. (1983) 'Purchasing must become supply base management', *Harvard Business Review*, **Sep/Oct**, 109–117

Lamming, R. (1993) *Beyond Partnership: Strategies for Innovation and Lean Supply*, Prentice Hall International, Hemel Hempstead

Nisiguchi, T. (1994) *Strategic Industrial Sourcing: The Japanese Advantage*, Oxford University Press, New York

Syson, R. (1992) *Improving Purchase Performance*, Pitman CIPS, Easton on the Hill

5 Strategic sourcing

Introduction

Chapter 4 showed how a reduced supply base of better quality suppliers may be achieved. An important part of this process was the identification of strategic areas of supply, using purchase portfolio analysis. These are products or services which, because of their high value, or degree of risk to the organization should there be a failure to supply to specified requirements, threaten the achievement of the organization's strategic objectives, or even its survival. This chapter examines how the organization's strategic sourcing needs may be met.

Thus the objectives of this chapter are to:

- Identify characteristics of competitive and partnership approaches to strategic sourcing.
- Illustrate the advantages of partnership for customer and supplier.
- Examine the applicability of partnership in various sectors.
- Explore the process of implementing strategic partnerships with suppliers.
- Identify success factors in partnership relationships.

Strategic sourcing options

Traditionally, relationships between buyers and suppliers in Europe and North America have been characterized as competitive or adversarial. More recently, however, the success of Japanese manufacturing companies has been attributed in part to the adoption of partnership relationships with their strategic suppliers. However, before you can determine whether partnership (or competition) is an appropriate option, you need to be able to distinguish the models. Researchers have identified various distinguishing characteristics of these approaches, which are set out in Table 5.1, and discussed below.

Supplier selection

This is the core function of purchasing, and the method used, whether tendering or negotiation, clearly distinguishes competitive and partnership approaches. Lamming (1993) equates closed, price-based competition and

Table 5.1
Procurement models and purchasing characteristics

Characteristic	Competition	Partnership
Supplier selection	Tendering	Negotiation
Contract duration	Short term	Long term
No. of suppliers	Many	One or two
Contractual relations	Very formal and rigid	Flexible and informal
Communications with suppliers	Very guarded and sporadic	Open and continuous
Negotiation	Win–lose	Win–win
Joint activities with suppliers	Little or none	Extensive
Attitude to quality	Incoming inspection	Continuous improvement
Delivery practice	Large quantity, infrequent	Small quantity, just-in-time
Systems	Manual, separate	Electronic, integrated

inviting bids from a wide range of sources with non-partnership models, whilst collaborative, negotiated selection of suppliers based upon performance is characteristic of partnership. Most organizations use a combination of methods for supplier selection, depending on the criticality of the items purchased. Thus you may use purchase portfolio analysis to help in distinguishing between strategic items, which would be appropriate for negotiation with single or dual source suppliers, and non-critical or leverage items, suppliers of which may be selected on price following formal tendering procedures.

Contract duration

The precise duration of contracts for distinguishing the models is open to conjecture, and may vary depending on the type of goods. For example, commodities are likely to be one-off, spot purchases to take advantage of market conditions, and commonly available low-technology items, such as stationery, for which there are many comparable suppliers, may be purchased on short-term contracts. By contrast, contracts for key components for a new car model or aeroplane may be for up to ten or fifteen years.

Number of suppliers

In the competitive approach, it is common practice to split contracts between several suppliers on a 'cherry-picking' basis. Rather than identifying the best overall deal from a single supplier, buyers will select the lowest bids against each item on a contract, the result being a greater number of suppliers to manage. Lamming found that dual sourcing is a common feature of partnership as practised in Japan, with single sourcing for strategic parts where there are no volume, variety or delivery constraints.

Contractual relations

Flexibility and informality of contractual relations is associated with partnership, whilst very formal and rigid contractual terms are associated with competition. The rationale for this is that partnership is based upon trust, and a developing relationship over time; therefore detailed provisions regarding the rights and responsibilities of parties, contractual disputes and claims are inappropriate.

Communications with suppliers

Irregular, paper-based communications are associated with a competitive buying approach, whilst continuous, electronic or verbal communications are a feature of partnership. Lamming characterizes partnership as two-way and long term, whilst information exchange in non-partnership models is very restricted, used as a weapon and is short term.

Joint activities with suppliers

In the partnership approach, there are many joint activities covering areas such as design, specification, cost improvement and joint financing, whilst in an extreme competitive approach, there would be few or no such joint activities.

Negotiation

The nature of negotiations vary from win–win in the partnership model, to win–lose or even lose–lose in the competitive model, where the analogy of a game or battle is appropriate rather than co-operation over planned price reductions, which characterizes partnership.

Attitude to quality

The traditional method of assuring quality through incoming inspection is associated with competition, whilst in partnership customers and suppliers jointly seek to eliminate the causes of defective parts or unsatisfactory services through continuous improvement activities (see Chapter 6 for a fuller discussion).

Delivery practice

Close partnership relations facilitate the introduction of just-in-time delivery of small quantities direct to the point of use, whilst competition implies infrequent deliveries of large quantities to build up large security stocks.

Systems

As suggested under Communications with suppliers above, paper-based trading is characteristic of competition, whilst suppliers and customers in a partnership are likely to develop full electronic trading, with financial, procurement, production and quality systems being integrated as closely as possible.

Whilst the partnership and competition approaches are presented as opposites, in practice your organization's relationships with its suppliers will fall in between the extremes of each characteristic. It is also likely that relationships with some suppliers will lie more towards the competitive end of the spectrum, and those with others will exemplify partnership to a greater extent. However, it is important that your organization has a clear rationale for its general policy on supplier relationships, as well as for conducting relations with suppliers of different products or in different markets in different ways.

INVESTIGATE

- *What is your organization's policy on supplier relationships? Using the above framework, how would you characterize the relationships with those suppliers with which you are involved? If there are differences in the nature of relationships with different suppliers, what is the rationale for this?*

Whilst the use of the word 'options' suggest that organizations have a free choice as to the nature of their relationships with suppliers, in practice there are many constraints. Perhaps the greatest is custom and practice, or organizational inertia, as a result of which traditional adversarial practices are maintained despite formal recognition of the benefits of partnership (see the example of the UK automobile industry given later in this chapter). There may also be constraints imposed by the sector within which the organization operates. Thus it is argued that in high-technology, highly competitive global markets, such as those for automobiles and consumer electronics, the only way to compete and survive is to adopt a partnership approach with suppliers of strategic products. In other markets which are more localized and where products have a lower technical content, such as construction, the adversarial approach may be appropriate, as the following extract indicates.

The Latham review of the UK construction industry

In 1993 the Government asked Sir Michael Latham to direct a joint government/industry review of procurement and contractual relationships in the UK construction industry.

Sir Michael's first report was presented to Department of the Environment ministers in December. His interim conclusions are that adversarial contractual attitudes and poor productivity are the most serious problems facing the UK construction industry and that these result in [it] being relatively uncompetitive in comparison with other industries in developed countries.

Source: Chartered Institute of Purchasing and Supply, The Latham Review, Pactum Serva, *p. 12, February 1994*

However, as the Mowlem case shows (see below), partnership is not unknown even in this sector.

In the public sector, competition is embodied in legislation, formal rules and procedures designed to ensure as far as possible the proper use of public funds, the achievement of value for money, and that potential suppliers are not discriminated against. In particular, the EC Directives on Public Procurement and UK legislation on Compulsory Competitive Tendering lay down formal procedures requiring selection by competitive tendering in most cases (see Chapter 8 for a fuller discussion). Such procedures, and the penalties associated with non-compliance, have tended to result in a reluctance to get too close to suppliers, and therefore made difficult any attempt to achieve the claimed benefits of partnership in the public sector. However, the following extract demonstrates that a mixed approach, partnership within competition, is advocated as an approach designed to meet the specific objectives of the public sector.

Public procurement policy: partnership within competition

15.3   In exercising its purchasing power, the Government has two fundamental aims:
   – Value for money.
   – Improving the competitiveness of its suppliers.

15.4   These aims are complementary. To win public contracts in competition, suppliers need to produce good quality, keenly priced goods and services. This is of mutual benefit to public sector customers, and the taxpayer, and to suppliers themselves who will be in a better position to win business internationally. Seeking value for money through competition contributes to a sound industrial and commercial base.

> 15.5 Equally helping suppliers through a constructive partnership, rather than a short-term arm's length, adversarial relationship, will lead to cost savings as well as improving quality and service delivery to the mutual benefit of both customer and supplier. Such a partnership needs to be established by competitive tender and reopened periodically to competition.
>
> *Source: Department of Trade and Industry*, White Paper on Competitiveness: Helping Business to Win (Cm 2563), *HMSO, London, p. 154, May 1994*

Partnership within competition is re-emphasized in the 1995 White Paper on government procurement strategy (Treasury, 1995), which states that there should be:

A continuing emphasis on fair competition, as being the cornerstone of good procurement, coupled with constructive co-operation between customers and suppliers. (Foreword)

The White Paper goes further in relation to highly specialized markets or complex and continuously developing requirements, stating that:

A longer term partnering arrangement will be appropriate . . . such arrangements will be established through competition and subject to further competition. (p. 13)

Closer and more continuous relationships with suppliers of services are also proposed (p. 17). Thus, there is increasing encouragement for public purchasers to adopt practices consistent with partnership within the constraints of competition and accountability.

Partnership sourcing

There is no doubt that the benefits of partnership are being increasingly recognized by academics and practitioners. Partnership Sourcing Ltd is a company set up by the Confederation of British Industry (CBI) with the support of the Department of Trade and Industry (DTI) to promote partnership. Partnership sourcing is defined as:

A commitment by customers/suppliers, regardless of size, to a long-term relationship based on clear mutually agreed objectives to strive for world-class capability and performance. (CBI, 1991)

Characteristics of partnership are identified as follows:

- Top level commitment.
- Openness and trust.
- Clear joint objectives between buyer and supplier.
- Long-term relationship.
- Proactive not reactive.
- Total quality management.
- Working together.
- Flexibility.
- Involvement of all disciplines.

The advantages for purchasers are:

- Faster product and service development.
- Improved quality.
- Delivery on time.
- Designing cost out.

For suppliers, the advantages are:

- Long-term-agreement.
- Improved management capability.
- Marketing advantage.
- Improved technological capability.
- Financial stability, including payment on time.

and the advantages for both parties are:

- Reduced total cost, profitable for both parties.
- Lower inventories and reduced logistics.

The following cases provide practical examples of the advantages of partnership claimed by Partnership Sourcing Ltd. Try to identify examples of the characteristics and advantages for purchasers and suppliers suggested by Partnership Sourcing Ltd. in these cases.

HD Plastics

At its Biggleswade factory, HD Plastics makes bin liners. With 250 employees, the plant operates 24 hours a day, producing 820 million bags a year from 15 500 tonnes of polymer. The company has successfully created good supplier relationships, and benefits from them in tangible business terms. In this, it has much to teach others. Corinne Butt is HD's manufacturing support manager:

'I want my suppliers to make a profit. If they don't, they can't reinvest and develop. But we don't expect them to waste our time if they can't fulfil our needs in terms of delivery, service, quality of design and commitment.

I never threaten my suppliers. I am always totally open with them. My attitude is simple. I tell them: this is the business that's available and somebody has got to supply us. It could be you or it could be somebody else. I'm not ruling you out, but the product must be right for our customers. I am only a middle man . . .'

Substantial savings

HD's work in building special relationships with suppliers has produced substantial savings in another area – this time transit packaging, now supplied by Amcor Performance Packaging.

Previously, HD bought its transit cartons from two companies. Butt, always on the look out for new suppliers who could offer a better deal, found one in Amcor. In mid-1989, Amcor was new to the UK. As Butt says:

'I know from experience that a new supplier just setting up will go through teething problems. I couldn't risk any failure to deliver. But Amcor was always at the back of my mind.'

The right approach

By spring 1991, Butt was ready to see an Amcor salesman. She was impressed:

'He briefed me on the company – where it came from, what it planned to do with its business. It was completely different from the approach of other potential suppliers. This man only wanted to tell me how his company could help mine. He concentrated on looking for solutions to business problems.'

A visit to Amcor's £24-million factory followed 2 weeks later:

'Amcor stood out as a professional company. Although it was marketing a seemingly low-tech commodity – cardboard boxes – the company was really switched on. The design effort that went into its purpose-built site was excellent.'

More to the point, Amcor carried out compression tests on HD's existing transit cartons and found that the company was overspecifying.

'It showed us how to produce a more substantial carton for 20 per cent less cost.'

A trial run with the new packaging followed with everybody pleased with the results.

The delivery came in on time. There were no difficulties with the paperwork and the product went out to our customers with no problems at all.

Source: Extracts from I. Vallely, 'I never threaten my suppliers', in DTI Boardroom Report: Best Practice in Purchasing, Findlay Publications, Horton Kirby, pp. 14–17, 1993

The main characteristics exemplified in this case are top level commitment, openness and trust, clear joint objectives and working together. The advantages demonstrated include reduced cost for both parties, delivery on time, and designing cost out.

Apollo Fire Detectors

Fasteners can be the bane of a buyer's life. Usually they represent less than 1% of a manufacturing company's total spend, but the range of fasteners and number of suppliers is vast – and the effort required to source all you need easily becomes disproportionate to their value. So when Apollo Fire Detectors of Havant first adopted partnership sourcing, it decided to start with one of its fastener suppliers, TR Fastenings of Uckfield.

That was 3 years ago when Apollo had a total of 800 suppliers providing 4000 different components – from nuts and bolts to custom-made mouldings and printed circuit boards that go to make up its fire detectors. Today, Apollo has 54 suppliers, and 95% of its £8 million annual spend is channelled through just 25 of them.

The logic behind Apollo's vendor rationalization programme was simple: to reduce costs and improve productivity, feeding the savings back into the organization in order to stabilize sales prices and increase its market share. The strategy appears to be working.

The company, with a £15 million annual turnover and 250 employees, continues to grow at the rate of 30% a year. Since adopting partnership sourcing, inventory value has been cut by at least a third, production no longer suffers from line shortages and expensive storage space has been put to better use.

Paul Domican is Apollo's materials manager:

'Partnership sourcing is part of our continuous improvement programme and it's played a major role in our success, but we've had to change our method of operation completely.'

These changes relate to Apollo's buying policy. Paul Domican's department used to be called Purchasing. Today, it is Materials Management. Although that change may appear superficial, it represents the real shift of emphasis that is necessary to make partnership sourcing work. Domican explains:

> 'Our function has developed from one of price negotiation and purchasing administration to becoming a cost-effective internal supplier. The improved productivity of the department also means that it has more time to communicate with suppliers on a strategic, long-term basis.'

And good communications, believes Domican, are absolutely central to the success of good, working relationships.

To Malcolm Diamond, group managing director of TR Fastenings, a second vital component is complete honesty:

> 'Partnership sourcing is all about working openly together to build a more competitive situation and at the same time reduce costs for both sides. If we are getting it wrong, we expect to be told. Likewise, if a customer's business is experiencing difficulties, we need to be told.'

Being completely open with a supplier about business plans will be alien to many buyers. But if your supplier is going to hold stocks, control deliveries and manage lead times from third parties, as well as control quality and costs, you must keep him informed. And that implies total trust.

Built on mutual trust

For TR and Apollo, partnership sourcing works. It is a relationship that is built entirely on mutual trust. There is no binding contract. But this is not a trading condition that can be reached overnight. It takes time.

TR used to bid for tenders at Apollo alongside other fastener suppliers. It took 3 years to change that to negotiating fixed prices for short-term periods, to orders limited by total spend, and eventually to open-value orders limited by quality of product.

Today, the two negotiate one price and Apollo issues a single order to cover the £300 000 worth of fasteners that it knows will be needed for the year ahead. This compares with around 200 separate orders that it would place with TR before partnership sourcing.

The savings for Apollo are substantial. TR delivers direct to the factory floor. There is no booking in or goods inward inspection. Stock levels are monitored by shopfloor personnel and they contact TR by fax when more is required. For TR, the benefit is more income. Previously, it shared Apollo's fastening business with four or five other suppliers.

However, close relationships, like that of Apollo and TR, do not preclude problems. Apollo's Domican explains: 'If any of our suppliers fail to meet competitive prices, quality or service standards, we let them know. We also retain the ultimate sanction of parting company at any time. That's unlikely to happen, having spent so long getting to know and trust one another.'

All round change

Partnership sourcing can provide long-term benefits for both parties but it demands that traditional buying methods and attitudes are changed. If a purchasing department's performance continues to be measured on unit costs, all that a supplier can do is keep cutting its prices. Being cheaper will get them noticed but the cheapest is not always the best. The effects of buying on price alone are short-term, short-sighted and self-defeating. Your supplier base will continue to grow, costs will continue to rise and quality will fly out of the window.

Source: Extracts from P. Nutton, 'It's played a major role in our success', DTI Boardroom Report: Best Practice in Purchasing, Findlay Publications, Horton Kirby, pp. 18-23, 1993

The main characteristics are again openness and trust (note the absence of a binding contract), working together and a long-term relationship. Good communications is also emphasized, which is not listed separately by Partnership Sourcing Ltd, but is clearly critical to success. The main advantages are again reduced cost with, in addition, lower inventories and improved logistics, leading to an apparent marketing advantage as seen in the growth of Apollo's business.

John Mowlem & Co. plc

The building business is notoriously litigious at the best of times, and these are hardly the best of times. Yet when other construction companies' response to the battle for survival is to squeeze ever more out of equally hard-pressed and insecure suppliers and sub-contractors, one company, John Mowlem & Co. plc, has adopted a more mature and far-sighted approach and is seeking to establish long-term alliances with its key vendors.

John Mowlem has a turnover of £1.5 billion in construction-related businesses of which 70% is represented by bought-in materials and subcontracts. Procurement generally is devolved to the individual business unit, which often means the individual construction site, co-ordinated by a very small group procurement unit of six people, most of whom have previously held senior procurement jobs in the divisions.

This unit, under director Mike Wallis, has overall direction of procurement.

Mr Wallis characterizes the traditional relationships in the industry as an unequal equation. 'You can't deliver something you haven't bought; for example you can't deliver quality if you've bought rubbish.'

So what do clients want? Mr Wallis, who has been in the 'client' position in his career, says that most important is on-time completion. Partnership relations lead to faster project completion because vendors can be brought on board quicker.

Pricing is also important, of course. Traditionally, and especially in recession, many in the construction industry have underpriced in the expectation of being able to claw back to a profit through extras and variations. This attitude doesn't let the main contractor deliver a fair price to the client. Mowlem is looking to deal with companies with a good record of managing their own prices.

Mowlem is also looking to work with companies who will do more than merely produce on time, to specification and to price. It is looking for firms prepared to make a creative input that will result in saving the client's money, but Mr Wallis says this will not come about if vendors don't realize that their investment in ideas will lead directly to further work in the future. Mr Wallis parallels this with his experience in the automotive industry, where partners are chosen by negotiation to participate from a very early point in the design stage, and he is trying to introduce a similar sort of early involvement and commitment to the construction industry.

The key to success, believes Mr Wallis, lies in information. Traditional attitudes are in part due to suppliers not knowing what's in the pipeline – from their point of view the current contract is the only contract. By operating an open door policy at the centre so that key vendors can discover what other work is likely to be available in the future, who the decision makers are, what innovations in technology or practice are likely to be required, the maximization of short-term profit site by site can be replaced by a more secure long-term growth of business for Mowlem and its suppliers. In addition to being briefed on what Mowlem sees as happening 2 or 3 years down the line, vendors can be offered assistance in improving their performance (for instance, help in qualifying for BS 5750) and the links between the supplier programme and Mowlem's related quality programme are close.

Since Mowlem's approach is based on the primacy of information, suppliers often have to invest in internal systems, but this once done, suppliers will find this of commercial advantage in dealing with other main contractors as well.

Not that Mowlem is some benevolent institution. The approach hasn't been adopted as part of a 'be nice to suppliers' campaign. Relations can still be blunt at site level, although the need for this should diminish if the right partners have been chosen. On

Mowlem sites co-operation is improved between the suppliers and contractor – a direct selling point for clients.

And it works, much to the amazement of many old hands in the industry, and not just externally but internally. Four years ago, says Mr Wallis, sister companies in the group were winning only perhaps 20% of the intragroup trade potentially open to them, again largely due to lack of information. Now Mr Wallis estimates that figure at more like 80%. Internally or externally, the buyers are still in control – indeed in these long-term relationships the buyers probably have greater control than hitherto – and the suppliers are working harder for Mowlem.

Disputes still occur, of course, but both sides are committed to try for realistic arbitration rather than reaching for lawyers (the construction industry generally spends more on litigation than it does on training). None of the agreements with key partners have been through the legal department – as Mr Wallis says, if one side is unhappy with an agreement it's pointless; if both sides are happy then lawyers are unnecessary. So far, Mowlem hasn't 'fallen out' with any key supplier, although a partnership is not a meal ticket for life. Tender lists also contain non-key suppliers, against whom partners' performance can be continually judged, but through Mowlem's monitoring of the relationship, partners can be encouraged and helped to stay ahead of the game.

Source: M. Wallis, 'Cementing relations', IFPMM, European Purchasing and Materials Management, Cornhill, London pp. 63–64, 1994

The main characteristics include long-term relationships, openness and trust, flexibility and team working. In addition, the importance of information, the supplier as a source of innovation, and service to the client are emphasized. Note again the lack of legal agreements. Advantages identified include faster service development reflected in better on-time completion, financial stability through better price management, and marketing advantage measured by business growth.

INVESTIGATE

- *Does your organization practise partnership with any of its suppliers? What are the main characteristics which distinguish the partnership from relations with other suppliers? What are the advantages and disadvantages of partnership relationships?*

As discussed above, partnership cannot be the solution to successful strategic sourcing for all sectors and all suppliers, but where appropriate and with carefully selected suppliers there is considerable evidence to support partnership sourcing. However, even in the automobile sector, where the benefits of partnership have been researched and demonstrated possibly more than in any other, a recent report found that true partnership was not being practised in the UK. Its author, Professor Richard Lamming of the University of Bath, has distinguished between partnership as practised in the Japanese automotive industry, and lean supply, which he suggests is more appropriate to European and North American manufacturers. Lean supply differs from Japanese partnership in that:

- Partnership is based upon the unique relationships in Japan between government, financial institutions, manufacturing companies and their suppliers.
- Partnership is unequal, in that manufacturers dominate the relationship with their suppliers.

In many other respects, however, lean supply is similar to partnership sourcing, though with an added emphasis on:

- Reducing the cost of components throughout the supply chain by improving internal processes and external logistics (lean production).
- Making maximum use of world class suppliers' technological edge to provide competitive advantage over competing companies (Lamming, 1993).

Professor Lamming was commissioned by the Society of Motor Manufacturers and Traders (SMMT) and the Department of Trade and Industry (DTI) to examine the extent to which lean supply was being practised in the UK automobile industry. His main findings are presented below.

Relationships between vehicle manufacturers and suppliers

The report concludes that the necessary levels of interfirm trust are not present in the industry for lean supply – and therefore comprehensive lean production – to become a reality. The mistrust which is in evidence is the result of many years of broken promises, abuse of confidence, and general acrimony within the industry. Some progress towards better relationships has been made but it is limited to a few firms. In developing new working agreements with their suppliers, most vehicle manufacturers still appear to deal more in rhetoric than reality.

Communications between vehicle manufacturers and their direct suppliers appears to be generally improved but still not at a level to support such imperatives as effective implementation of electronic data interchange or collaboration on product and process development. Where vehicle manufacturers practise 'supplier development' there is often a sense of dogma and domination by the customer, with suppliers unable to explain that the process could be much improved by two-way communication.

The industry structure is apparently not yet moving towards tiering – in which responsibilities for logistics and technology are shared between firms at different levels. Nevertheless, the expressions first-tier and second-tier are used widely – an abuse of terminology which may be delaying genuine industrial development. The technical abilities of component suppliers are still underutilized, partly as a result of territorial protection within the vehicle manufacturers. This appears to be especially prevalent in the area of outsourcing responsibility for component design and specification.

The concept of supplier associations – informal groupings within supply chains aimed at improving logistics and technical factors through collaboration – is becoming established and suppliers appear to view the idea as generally practical. This and other approaches are necessary for a spread of shared learning on lean supply practices in order to benefit the industry as a whole.

There is a proliferation of approaches to supplier assessment, leading to confusion and frustration for component firms: some degree of common approach is necessary to remove the waste of effort currently borne by suppliers. The future of this technique may lie in relationship assessment – genuine collaboration in joint assessment of efficient supply chains.

Open-book negotiation is in general use within the industry – especially between vehicle manufacturers and their direct suppliers – but the more collaborative technique of cost transparency (requiring both customer and supplier to share sensitive information) has yet to be developed.

Most suppliers are using benchmarking to assess their productivity, including European Community and global comparisons. Indirect (second-tier) suppliers are using this less and there is a danger of their optimizing to sub-world-class levels of performance.

Raw material suppliers (metals, chemicals, etc.) appear to be unwilling to adopt lean supply practices with their automotive customers (who are often small component manufacturers) and are seen as a barrier to development of better logistics management. Some joint action by vehicle manufacturers and possibly pressure from SMMT/DTI is necessary to change this situation.

There is little formal preparation for the requirements of BS 7750 – the new British Standard concerning environmental soundness in supply chains. A much better awareness of environmental management needs to be stimulated in the components industry.

The SMMT has several projects underway which, if successful, might improve a number of the problems in the industry – especially those requiring better collaboration between firms. Such initiatives deserve full support and effective dissemination in order to help the industry move to a different nature – one of joint exploitation of mutual benefits and improved prosperity.

Source: R. Lamming, A Review of Relationships between Vehicle Manufacturers and Suppliers, The DTI/SMMT Automotive Components Supplier Initiative Stage Two, *Department of Trade and Industry, London, p. 5, February 1994*

The report therefore suggests that there are considerable difficulties in implementing lean supply or partnership in sectors and countries where adversarial relationships have traditionally been dominant. For example, it was suggested above that there were constraints on introducing the partnership or lean supply approaches to the public sector. Can you identify those features which would and would not be relevant or applicable?

Features which are relevant:
- Concentration on core business, with contracting out of non-core activities to technically superior suppliers of services and processes, e.g. facilities management and logistics, thereby reducing overheads.
- 'Cost-down' initiatives, though not necessarily on the basis of two-way access to financial information.
- Increasing use of buying agencies, e.g. HMSO, The Buying Agency. (formerly Crown Suppliers), and local authority buying consortia such as the Yorkshire Purchasing Organization, which supply not just products but *expertise* in buying.
- In healthcare purchasing, provider Trusts, especially acute hospitals, will increasingly offer innovation and expertise in specialist treatments, e.g. transplant surgery and hip replacements, and collaborate with purchasing authorities on cost improvement activities.
- Public sector buyers could increasingly expect suppliers to take the initiative on cost improvement.

Features not relevant or applicable:
- Absence of financial investment in suppliers, although the Government's Private Finance Initiative seeks to attract private sector investment to major capital projects, e.g. the Channel Tunnel Rail Link.
- Long-term relationships with individual public sector organizations are not guaranteed due to the requirement for periodic competitive tendering; however, suppliers may have a long-term relationship

with parts of the public sector, so that if they lose one contract, they may gain others, e.g. providing refuse services to local authorities, or high-technology equipment to hospital Trusts.

● Collaboration with suppliers in setting strategic objectives, e.g. the scope of outsourcing and early involvement in design, is restricted by political, ethical and legal constraints.

The above examples show that partnership approaches may be applicable in sectors where the consensus view suggests they may not be. Thus it is of critical importance that you can assess the relevance and applicability of partnership features to the sector or organization in which you work, and the products or services for which you are responsible, rather than accept unquestioningly the claims for its superiority over other approaches.

Implementing strategic partnership

Moving to such a strategic sourcing arrangement is a major step for the organization, and one on which decisions will be taken at a senior level, with considerable prior planning and analysis. Purchasing staff may not even be involved until a late stage, especially where the potential partners are both major international corporations in their own right, and the partnership involves massive joint investment. There are many examples of this in the automobile sector, with alliances between Japanese and European and North American manufacturers, such as Rover and Honda in the UK (before Rover was taken over by BMW), and Ford and Mazda, General Motors and Toyota in the USA. As the above cases show, however, partnership can be practised by organizations of any size, and all purchasing staff can acquire an understanding of the process of implementing partnership, and the skills required to operate it successfully.

How many suppliers?

A key issue in assessing competitiveness and risk is whether to source strategic components or services from one or more partnership suppliers. Partnership does not automatically imply single sourcing; dual sourcing, perhaps with an unequal split, allows the development of an alternative supplier should the major partner fail, and also provides a degree of competition between the suppliers.

Leenders et al. (1989, pp. 257–259) identify arguments for both options. These may usefully be divided into constraints and advantages, indicating that a free choice may not be available.

Single supplier sourcing

Constraints:
- Prior commitments to long-term agreements.
- Exclusive ownership of a product or patent by a supplier.
- Smallness of the order precluding its division.
- Requirement for specific tooling which it would be expensive for more than one supplier to develop.

Advantages:
- Price or freight discounts.
- Supplier goodwill.
- Easier scheduling of deliveries.
- Fewer suppliers to manage.

Multisupplier sourcing

Constraints:
- Government regulations, e.g. favouring small business.
- The strategic nature of the product.
- Insufficient capacity of any one supplier to meet organizational demand.
- The need to test the performance of new suppliers before committing totally to one source.

Advantages:
- Keener competition for all suppliers.
- Assurance of supply should one source fail.
- Avoidance of supplier dependence on the organization with a consequent threat to its survival if orders are not forthcoming.

Before committing to single source supply, you need to assess its potential impact on competitiveness and security of supply of critical products. The short- and long-term effects of loss of continuity of supply also need to be assessed, and alternative potential sources of supply clearly identified. As part of the analysis, you might identify possible scenarios for interruption to supply, and calculate the costs to the organization to set against the potential benefits arising from single sourcing.

INVESTIGATE

- *Does your organization practise single or dual sourcing in respect of critical strategic supplies? What are the reasons for doing so, and are there constraints*

disadvantage

which limit your choice? Are there any areas of supply where current practice needs
to be reviewed?

What are the costs of developing partnerships?

Acquisition costs of new partnership suppliers will be considerable, including the 'soft' costs of building trust over a period of years as well as the
'hard' costs, such as those of aligning supply, ordering and invoicing systems. The need to develop a mutual understanding of the partners' strategic
aims, culture and processes, essential for the development of trust, implies a
considerable investment of staff time and expertise from top management
level down throughout the organization. Purchasing staff, in particular, will
need to liaise very closely with the design, production, marketing and
accounting departments of the partner. There may also be close involvement
with the partner's own purchasing department, to ensure that partnership
practices are carried out with their suppliers, or on the other hand to learn
from their greater experience of partnering. Supplier development activities
(see Chapter 6) will also require a considerable investment.

'Hard' costs may include establishing electronic data interchange links,
which implies a considerable cost in hardware, software and staff expertise,
and may involve short-term disruption and duplication of existing manual
systems. Production and logistics processes may need to be altered, with
possible new capital investment to facilitate lean production and just-in-
time delivery.

Against these costs, the benefits should be seen in: the reduction or
removal of clerical processes such as manual requisitioning, ordering, invoicing, checking deliveries against orders; ending the duplication of quality
assessment; savings from improved production and delivery; and the whole
process of organizational learning by both partners, which results in continuous cost and process improvement.

Do you need a contract?

It is argued that detailed contracts are unnecessary in a partnership, as the
all-embracing, flexible nature of the relationship is impossible to capture in a
legal document. The basis of trust may also be undermined by the minutiae
of contractual provisions, especially in respect of breach, which may often
become the basis for very adversarial negotiation. On the other hand, totally
informal, unwritten agreements may be very risky, especially if you are the
weaker party to a partnership. As a result, the concept of a partnership
contract, or loose-framework agreement, has been identified as a compromise. This would outline the respective responsibilities of the parties in
general terms, sharing of risks and rewards, rights of ownership where
there is joint investment, and procedures for review and termination within
agreed time-scales. The partnership contract may be reinforced by contracts
relating to specific orders. However, the practice of partnership outside
Japan is to date insufficiently developed and researched to be able to identify

best practice accurately. There is clearly a need for some protection, given the consequences for one of the parties of unforeseen events, such as the take-over of Rover by BMW and the subsequent threat to Honda's investment. How loose and informal the framework can be, and yet still provide the minimum level of protection acceptable, remains to be established.

Implementing partnership: Ellram's model

A managerial guideline for the development of partnerships is provided by Ellram (1991). Ellram identifies five phases, as presented in Figure 5.1. The evolution through the phases is summarized below.

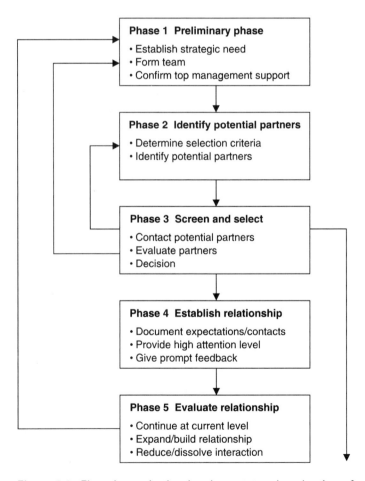

Figure 5.1 Five phases in the development and evaluation of purchasing partnerships. (From L. M. Ellram, 'A managerial guideline for the development and implementation of purchasing partnerships', *International Journal of Purchasing and Materials Management*, **27**(3), 2–8)

Phase 1: Preliminary phase

First, identification of the need for partnership as part of the organization's strategic plan. Second, a team representing key functional areas works on the development of the partnership. Third, top management support must be confirmed.

Phase 2: Identify potential partners

First, determine the selection criteria, and then identify potential partners. Selection criteria may include: cultural compatibility, long-term plans, financial stability, technology/design capability, top management compatibility, location, local laws and tariffs (with foreign partners), plant visits.

Phase 3: Screen and select

Potential suppliers are rated against the selection criteria, and their commitment to partnership, capability and cost structure for supplying the required item(s) are identified. Further consideration of the most promising suppliers may include detailed financial and operating analysis, plant visits and perceived availability, quality and overall 'fit'. Selection should not be dominated by any single criterion, but should seek an overall balance between them.

Phase 4: Establish the relationship

The partners' expectations of the relationship should be documented to prevent misunderstandings. The document could include key contacts, shared technology, handling of proprietary information, frequency of forecast updates, basis for price changes, etc. Purchasing should provide a central co-ordinating function, with regular team meetings to evaluate performance. Frequent interaction at all levels should take place, especially between senior managers of the partners to demonstrate commitment.

Phase 5: Evaluate relationships

After an initial period of up to 12 months, the performance of the partnership may be evaluated, with possible outcomes being: maintain at the present level; further build or expand the relationship; or dissolve or reduce the scope of the relationship. The latter option should not be taken lightly, as potential future partners may be deterred if suppliers are abandoned for no good reason.

Selection of the right partners is clearly critical. Cousins (1992) has developed a mathematically based computerized vendor selection model using 10 vendor selection criteria: price, delivery, quality, level of technology, culture, commerciality, productive flexibility, ease of communication and current reputation. The buyer weights these attributes by assigning appropriate points reflecting the importance attached to each. Then intensive discussions take place with potential suppliers and the data obtained is fed into the model, which calculates the most suitable partner for long-term relations.

Relationship assessment

A key feature of Ellram's approach and that of many other researchers is the emphasis on the importance of the relationship between supplier and customer, in particular that potential partners should have a high degree of cultural affinity. This is reflected in the relationship positioning tool in the Supply Chain Management Group's model, which is discussed more fully in Chapter 6. One aspect of the model of particular relevance here is assessment of the customer's attitude to the supplier under the following headings.

- *Business.* Does the customer appreciate the need to look at more than just the unit price and work with the supplier in trying to reduce costs? Does the customer allow the supplier to share the benefits of a successful relationship?
- *Commitment.* Is there a long-term commitment to the supplier by the customer?
- *Involvement.* Does the customer involve the supplier in decision-making processes? Is there a real attempt to develop an open relationship?
- *Dependency.* Is the customer's desire for a closer, long-term relationship backed up by policies which mean that the supplier is a genuine stakeholder in the customer's business? (Macbeth and Ferguson, 1994).

Other aspects of the model, such as information flows between customer and supplier, and vice versa, and how both partners organize, train and use their people resource, assess the strength of the mutual relationship, and identify areas where improvements need to be made.

The application of such a relationship assessment model as part of the process of establishing a partnership sourcing arrangement may be critical to its success. The next section examines success factors in a partnership relationship.

Success factors in strategic partnerships

The high investment demanded by partnership requires that success needs to be demonstrated and monitored, and that, where the partnership is not performing, or has reached the end of its useful life, it may be terminated without catastrophic consequences for both partners. We have seen that in the public sector periodic testing against the market is prescribed, and benchmarking (see Chapter 10) is practised by many companies in the private sector to assess the performance of partnership relationships against industry best practice or specific world class companies.

Partnership Sourcing Ltd suggest that the following factors should be measured in order to determine the success of a partnership:

- Relationships and attitudes.
- Reducing total cost.
- Meeting profit.
- Competitive position.
- Investment and technology.
- Flexibility.
- Communications.
- Quality.
- Logistics management.
- Innovation and value added.

The difficulty of assessing overall performance in purchasing is considered in Chapter 10, and is reflected in the above factors. For some of these, such as profit and reducing costs, there may be objective, quantitative data to measure the success of the partnership. For others, however, such as flexibility and attitudes, there may only be qualitative, subjective data, reflected in the feelings of key actors in both customer and supplier organization. A balanced assessment of both subjective and objective data therefore needs to be maintained.

Predicting partnership success

Given the costs and risk associated with the development of partnership, the value of a method of predicting its likely success could be enormous. Mohr and Spekman (1994) provide such a method based upon relationships between manufacturers and dealers in the personal computer industry. They attempt to correlate characteristics of partnership success based upon the following attributes with specified success factors:

Attributes of the partnership

- *Commitment*: willingness to exert effort on behalf of the relationship.
- *Co-ordination*: understanding of the set of tasks each party expects the other to perform.
- *Interdependence*: any loss of autonomy will be equitably compensated by mutual gains.
- *Trust*: the belief that the word of both parties is reliable and that they will fulfil their obligations.

Communication behaviour

- *Quality*: accuracy, timeliness, adequacy and credibility of information exchanged.
- *Information sharing*: extent to which critical, often proprietary information is communicated to one's partner.
- *Participation*: extent to which partners engage jointly in planning and goal setting.

Conflict resolution techniques

Given that conflicts may be expected in any relationship, how they are resolved has implications for partnership success. The methods examined are:

- Joint problem solving.
- Persuasion.
- Smoothing.
- Domination.
- Harsh words.
- Arbitration.

The measures of success against which the above attributes were tested are:

- Dealer sales volume of the partner's product.
- Percentage of total monthly sales of the dealership constituted by the partner's product.
- Satisfaction with profit and margins.
- Satisfaction with manufacturer support.

The research showed that co-ordination, commitment, communication quality, information sharing, participation, joint problem solving, and avoiding the use of smoothing over problems or severe resolution tactics were positively associated with partnership success. Interdependence, and persuasive tactics as a method to resolve conflict were found not to be predictors of partnership success (Mohr and Spekman 1994, p. 145).

More generally, research has shown that partnership works when:

- There is mutual recognition or risk and joint ownership.
- Benefits are measurable and mutual.
- Strategy has been fully researched.
- Business survival depends upon it.
- There are no or few surprises (cf. the Rover/Honda/BMW case).
- There are regular, effective communications at all levels.
- Responsibilities are specified in partnership contracts.
- Top management is closely involved.
- The partner provides added value.

- It is focused on key products or services.
- Commitment to total continuous improvement exists.

Problems with partnership

- Difficulty of identifying suitable suppliers.
- It will be time consuming, especially early on.
- Confidentiality and over dependence.
- Risks of single sourcing.
- Complacency bred from success.
- Impatience for results.
- Partnership may not be practised by suppliers with their suppliers.
- Unequal power and unequal distribution of benefits.
- How and when to terminate the partnership?

Summary

This chapter has examined strategic sourcing, in particular through partnership, which is the approach recommended by most commentators and official reports, and the benefits of which are demonstrated in cases involving not just major international corporations, but also small UK companies. However, partnership may not be appropriate to all sectors and goods and services purchased, and should be based upon analysis of the aims and sourcing strategies of the organization. Key issues in implementing partnership have been identified, and a framework presented which may assist in planning the process. The importance of relationships between partners has also been emphasized. Factors determining success in partnership have been suggested, with reference to a predictive model which may be used to monitor the development and benefits of the relationship.

Activities

1   You have been asked to present an analysis of your organization's suppliers of strategic goods and services in terms of whether you are practising competition or partnership. Use the characteristics listed in Table 5.1 to carry out the analysis.

2   Your Managing Director recently attended a Partnership Sourcing seminar, and has asked you to examine how it may be implemented in your organization. Write a paper outlining briefly the costs and benefits of partnership, the process by which it may be implemented in your organization, and how its success may be judged.

References and further reading

Confederation of British Industry (1991) *Partnership Sourcing*, CBI, London

Confederation of British Industry (1992) *Making Partnership Sourcing Happen*, CBI, London

Confederation of British Industry (1993) *Partnership Sourcing in the Service Sector*, CBI, London

Cousins, P. (1992) 'Choosing the right partner', *Purchasing and Supply Management*, **Mar.**, 21–23

Cox, A. W. and Lamming, R. C. (eds) (1994) *Strategic Procurement Management in the 1990s: Concepts and Cases*, Earlsgate Press, Winteringham

Department of Trade and Industry/Partnership Sourcing (1993) *Boardroom Report: Best Practice in Purchasing*, Findlay Publications, Horton Kirby

Ellram, L. M. (1991) 'A managerial guideline for the development and implementation of purchasing partnerships', *International Journal of Purchasing and Materials Management*, **27** (3), 2–8

Erridge, A. and Nondi, R. (1994) 'Public procurement: competition and partnership', *European Journal of Purchasing and Supply Management*, **1** (3), 169–180

Griffiths, F. (1992) 'Alliance partnership sourcing – a major tool for strategic procurement', *Purchasing and Supply Management*, **May**, 35–40

International Federation of Purchasing and Materials Management (1994) *European Purchasing and Materials Management*, Cornhill, London

Lamming, R. (1993) *Beyond Partnership: Strategies for Innovation and Lean Supply*, Prentice Hall International, Hemel Hempstead

Leenders, M. R., Fearon, H. E. and England, W. B. (1989) *Purchasing and Materials Management*, Irwin, Homewood, IL

Macbeth, D. K. (1994) 'The role of purchasing in a partnering relationship', *European Journal of Purchasing and Supply Management*, **1** (1), 19–26

Macbeth, D. K. and Ferguson, N. (1994) *Partnership Sourcing: An Integrated Supply Chain Approach*, Financial Times/Pitman, London

Mannion, D. (1994) 'Performance measurement: people, purchasing, partnership', *Purchasing and Supply Management*, **Jan.**, 34–36

Mohr, J. and Spekman, R. (1994) 'Characteristics of partnership success: partnership attributes, communication behavior, and conflict resolution techniques', *Strategic Management Journal*, **15**, 135–142

Presutti, W. D. (1992) 'The single source issue: US and Japanese sourcing strategies', *International Journal of Purchasing and Materials Management*, **28** (1)

Stuart, F. I. (1993) 'Supplier partnerships: influencing factors and strategic benefits', *International Journal of Purchasing and Materials Management*, **29** (4), 22–28

Treasury (1995) *Setting New Standards: A Strategy for Government Procurement*, Cm 2840, HMSO, London

Further information

Partnership Sourcing Ltd may be contacted at the CBI London Office at Centre Point (Tel. 0171 379 7400, ext. 2715)

Supply Chain Management Group, 59 Southpark Avenue, Glasgow G12 8LF, UK (Tel. 0141 330 5696)

6 Improving supplier performance

Introduction

Chapter 5 identified a range of relationships between customers and suppliers with a competitive, adversarial approach at one extreme and an ideal form of partnership at the other. Within all these relationships supplier performance is critical, but different methods may be used to maintain and improve it. Thus, in respect of quality, it is suggested that in adversarial relationships incoming inspection is used, whilst in partnership relationships the supplier, and their suppliers, take on the responsibility of ensuring as near to zero defects as is possible. Similarly, in a competitive selection approach, with frequent retendering largely on the basis of price, the customer relies on competition between potential suppliers to ensure satisfactory performance, and therefore does not place a high priority on working directly with the supplier to improve their performance. By contrast, a partnership supplier is long term, may be the sole source, and its product may be critical to the success of the customer. In such circumstances, there are strong incentives for the customer to invest time and expertise in developing the supplier in order to improve the performance of the relationship and to learn from the supplier's own experience.

The appropriate methods for improving supplier performance may also vary depending upon the nature of the product or service supplied. Components with a high technical content or with high risk associated with failure, such as those for an aircraft engine, may need years of joint research and development and testing to establish a high probability of zero defects before they are put into operation. Suppliers of less critical components, such as fabrics for seat coverings, may be required to achieve specified standards on only one occasion, and will be subject to less frequent monitoring. Monitoring of suppliers of services may be different again, as perceptions of service performance, such as with office cleaning, may be more important than quantitative measures.

This chapter, therefore, examines a range of methods of monitoring and improving supplier performance without preconception as to the ideal type of relationship between customer and supplier, as any or all of them may be appropriate with particular suppliers at different times.

The objectives of this chapter are to:

- Examine areas where improvements may be obtained, specifically cost, quality and delivery.

- Explore methods of monitoring supplier performance through quality standards, vendor rating and quality awards.
- Identify various ways of achieving improvements in supplier performance through close relationships, supplier associations and supplier development.

Where can improvement be achieved?

The easy answer is that virtually any aspect of cost, quality, delivery and the overall business relationship may be improved, no matter how good or bad current performance is. The critical factor is whether there is the commitment on both sides of the relationship to improve. It was suggested in Chapter 5 that a mutual commitment to continuous improvement was a critical success factor in partnership. Equally, in a competitive selection situation, the current supplier's performance will be influenced by the desire to retain the business when it is retendered.

Cost

It is important to note the difference between price and cost at this stage. Price is what the supplier is prepared to accept for the provision of supplies or services. It includes the supplier's own purchasing costs, costs of production or performing the service, and may include delivery to a specified location. The supplier then adds a percentage profit to make up the price at which he is prepared to sell. This may then become the subject of negotiation, and in adversarial relationships the buyer may have to engage in the courtship ritual of bargaining, based upon educated guesswork as to what the supplier's bottom price is. Costs in this scenario are fixed, and suppliers would normally not be prepared to supply at below actual cost unless they are seeking to enter a market, challenge a competing supplier on price, or do not know their real costs (in which case you would probably be wise not to do business with them). Negotiation on price, therefore, does not necessarily result in improved supplier performance.

The case presented below illustrates the use of price/cost analysis in a competitive tendering situation, not merely to second guess the suppliers' prices, but also to ensure that their prices are not so low as to threaten their survival and, consequently, continuity of supply.

Purchase cost control in British Gas

National contracts are set up over 1–3 or 5 years, depending upon the product and availability. There can be benefits in long-term contracts if they are competitively priced. There is not a lot to be gained by changing the supplier. We would only go out to tender in the initial phase, but will use the Purchase Cost Control (PCC) department. They set targets for a product, which enables us to gauge tenders against a realistic price, and prevents predatory pricing by the supplier. Once a fair and reasonable price is decided, a price adjustment formula is established based on the PCC economists' estimates using available indices to gauge trends in products. This together with cost analysis creates a formula for price control, and prevents the supplier increasing prices unreasonably, especially in a single source situation. In other areas where we go out to tender more frequently, e.g. for meter boxes or governors, there is a tendency for suppliers to undercut one another's prices, ending up with a price that is too low. We would quiz the manufacturers to see if they can still remain viable at the price offered, because we would prefer to deal with companies that are still going to be around in 25 years' time. It's not a good idea to enforce a keen price scenario because it may have consequences for security of supply.

Source: Interview with Purchasing Manager, National Supplies, British Gas

Whilst the above illustration relates to offer prices in an adversarial situation, encouraging suppliers to examine and reduce their costs, often as part of a supplier development programme (see below), can result in improvements which should benefit both customer and supplier. They may also be extended to the supplier's suppliers to reduce costs throughout the supply chain. Hines (1994, pp. 31–32) argues that the 'build up of costs runs all the way from raw material source to final delivery and sale to the end user', and may even include the cost of disposal.

Hines argues that the traditional methods available for measuring cost, such as standard costing, are not entirely satisfactory or appropriate to the concept of continuous cost improvement. Standard costing is often based on inaccurate and dated information, with overhead costs allocated arbitrarily, and does not effectively predict costs or help companies target non-value-added areas. He distinguishes five alternative approaches:

- *Activity-based costing*: concerned with a more equitable allocation of overhead costs.
- *Throughput accounting*: concerned with maximizing throughput in a factory, i.e. sales revenue minus direct material costs, ignoring fixed costs.

Hines argues that a combination of these approaches would not only help to identify non-value-adding activities on the factory shop floor but would also make areas for improvement in indirect costs more visible.

- *Functional analysis*: the cost of a product is broken down into the different functions that a product demonstrates; each function is then analysed, alternative methods are evaluated and costed to identify the most cost-effective method.
- *Target costing*: maximum allowable costs are established before the start of production for each stage of a product's life cycle as defined by customer requirements. Costs are at their highest at the start of production, and are targeted to fall through improvements in the design and production process.
- *Kaizen costing*: this method periodically re-examines target costs after the start of production, and aims to achieve continuous cost reduction through the analysis of bought-in goods and materials, production processes, transportation, labour and other fixed overhead costs.

The last three approaches are almost entirely confined to Japanese companies, and are often combined to achieve a very effective cost projection and monitoring mechanism. This is applied throughout the supply chain to several tiers of suppliers as well as the manufacturer's own processes. It therefore implies a totally open analysis of customers' and suppliers' costs and profit levels, and a mutual commitment to work together to reduce costs without sacrificing customer requirements. As such, it is totally at odds with the price-based bargaining scenario outlined above, which is still common in relationships between customers and suppliers outside Japan. The Ford case presented below illustrates the difficulty that a UK manufacturer has in catching up with their Japanese competitors' cost improvement activities.

Cost improvement in Ford UK

Once the best quality supplier has been chosen, we look for a real reduction in price over the years. We would look for a 1% reduction in price in real terms per year. It is difficult for some suppliers, especially for commodities such as aluminium. However, the Japanese go for a 5% reduction, so how can we compete? It's a matter of improving the whole business. We have lost 50% of our staff over the last 10 years. We now have about 12 000 staff, but the Japanese do it with 5000. They would have 300 staff in an engine plant, where we have 3000.

Source: Interview, Procurement Planning Manager, Ford UK

Cost reduction in Rolls Royce Aerospace

Rolls Royce set itself a more ambitious target in 1989 of reducing the cost for purchases by 25% by 1992–93. This required the company to:

- Develop a single point of contact with suppliers.
- Establish a longer term commitment to suppliers.
- React positively to supplier ideas.
- Support supplier development.
- Develop a material requirements planning system.

Actions required by suppliers were:

- Cost reduction initiatives and innovation.
- Development of manufacturing capabilities.
- Investment in capital equipment.
- To adopt a total quality approach (see below).

Source: Interview, Purchasing Manager, Rolls Royce

You should therefore be aware of how you may encourage suppliers and your own colleagues to take advantage of opportunities for reducing your mutual costs through collaborative efforts. The improvement areas outlined below will not be the sole responsibility of purchasing staff, but you should be involved as part of teams in most of them.

INVESTIGATE

- *Does your organization seek to assess suppliers' costs, and if so, how? Are the costing methods suggested by Hines, and the two-way, open-book approach implied, relevant to your relationship with suppliers?*

Quality

Quality costs in a manufacturing environment are identified by the British Standards Institution (1990) as follows:

- *Prevention costs*: the costs of any action taken to investigate, prevent or reduce defects and failures.
- *Appraisal costs*: the costs of assessing the quality achieved.
- *Internal failure costs*: the costs arising within the manufacturing organization of failure to achieve the quality specified (before transfer of ownership to the customer).

- *External failure costs*: the costs arising outside the manufacturing organization of failure to achieve the quality specified (after the transfer of ownership to the customer).

Apart from external failure costs, these are costs to the supplier, but the customer may also be incurring costs under the first two headings through the need to duplicate inspection on delivery, and to maintain a supplier quality assessment system. Costs arising from quality failure could take any or all of the following forms:

- Loss of production time whilst waiting for replacement parts of the correct quality.
- Delays to new product development programmes.
- High goods inward inspection costs, and reinspection of stock after defects discovered.
- Return of defective supplies together with the generation of associated paperwork and disputes over responsibility.
- The need to recall products found to be defective.
- Claims from end customers under warranty, or for damages should defective parts be found to cause accident and injury.
- Ultimately, loss of customers because of a poor record on quality and reliability.

Clearly, therefore, investment in prevention and appraisal is preferable to rectification of faults later in the process, as demonstrated below in the case of Lucas Brakes.

Improving supplier quality in Lucas Brakes, Cwmbran

With a little help from their computer system, buyers at Lucas's brake factory at Cwmbran have secured a major improvement in their suppliers' quality levels. In the twelve months to October 1994, the proportion of goods received which were rejected fell to 2500 ppm. And the number of concessions – goods received out of specification but accepted into production – fell more than five-fold. 'We're confident that by prevention rather than detection we can achieve zero defects,' says Purchasing Agent Martyn Brown. To improve their monitoring of supplier performance, Buyers at Cwmbran developed a system on an IBM relational database. It can generate a wide range of comparative reports. Assessing quality levels, it can compare one supplier against another, one supplier against commodity or industry standard performance; it can compare suppliers by a particular item; it can immediately generate virtually any report a buyer wants, covering any time period required. 'The system is providing us with the type of information that we and our suppliers need to achieve zero defects,' says Brown. We now communicate performance data electronically to our suppliers on a monthly basis advising them of progress towards their agreed ppm targets. 'It helps us and our quality engineers to focus on the real problem areas.'

Source: Department of Trade and Industry, Getting the Best from Your Supply Partners, Managing in the '90s, *DTI Publications, London, p. 13, 1995*

Macbeth and Ferguson (1994, p. 48) estimate that, in manufacturing, direct quality costs can add up to 30% of sales turnover to total costs, with additional indirect costs being incurred. It is clearly worthwhile therefore to understand what quality is and how it may be assured. Various characteristics or dimensions of quality may be identified, which indicate that the concept of quality is so multifaceted that narrow definitions or single methods of prevention, such as inspection, cannot capture its complexity. Macbeth and Ferguson's characterization of quality features is set out in Box 6.1.

Box 6.1 *Features of quality*

Performance
Detailed functions performed by the product or service. The following are further aspects of performance:

- *Features*: additional aspects of the product or service which differentiate it from those offered by competitors
- *Aesthetics*: special artistic or fashionable features
- *Reliability*: length of time for which the product can be expected to function without failure
- *Durability*: time dimension over which the product has to be reliable

Loss of function
The following relate to additional contact with suppliers when function is lost or degraded in some way:

- *Serviceability*: ease of maintenance, fault diagnosis and repair
- *Response time*: delay between trying to make contact, establishing what is to be done and actually completing the process
- *Personal treatment*: the way in which customer-contact people behave when customers contact the system

Internal aspects of quality
These aspects will only be perceived indirectly by customers:

- *Flexibility of the production system*: to respond to changes in customer requirements
- *Conformance to specification*: the minimum need to satisfy at least those criteria which have been amenable to precise quantification, usually at the design stage
- *Value*: the process through which customers go in evaluating whether the delivered quality justifies the price they are paying for the product or service
- *Perceived quality*: others' perceptions of a suppliers' products or services which influence potential customers' attitudes and expectations

Source: Extracts from D. K. Macbeth and N. Ferguson, Partnership Sourcing: An Integrated Supply Chain Approach, *Financial Times/Pitman, London, pp. 38–40, 1993*

Given the range of characteristics of quality, it is only to be expected that a wide range of quantitative and qualitative techniques need to be employed for its assessment. Dale's (1994, p. 5) categorization relates to the evolution of ideas about quality, and is presented in Figure 6.1.

Dale argues that as the focus of quality becomes progressively broader and more strategic with the move towards total quality management (TQM), so the reliance on tools and techniques is supplemented by an organization-wide approach to quality through involving, caring for and empowering

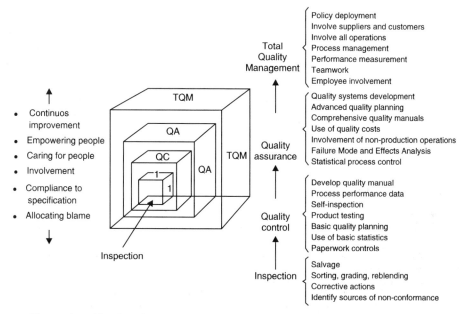

Figure 6.1 The four levels in the evolution of quality management. Reproduced from *Managing Quality* edited by Barrie Dale, by permission of the publisher, Prentice Hall International, Hemel Hempstead, 1994, p. 5)

people, leading to continuous improvement. For a clear and practical discussion of various aspects of quality, as well as techniques such as statistical process control and failure mode and effects analysis, see Bell et al. (1994).

The following case relates to a company which recognized it was losing orders partly due to the lack of a clear focus on quality. Which of the techniques for improving quality set out in Figure 6.1 can you identify?

Total quality management in Dowty

The problem: Dowty is the aerospace 'arm' of TI Group plc, whose core products are mechanical fuel metering systems, pumps and actuating systems, as well as the gas turbine engines that power commercial and military aircraft.

Despite its high reputation the company's management were complacent and the customers dissatisfied. The company failed to win significant business on the European Fighter because it did not listen to its customers. (Managing director Tony Bellisario believes that, although a major blow at the time, it was the catalyst for change.) It was critical to get back on course. But how?

The solution: A total quality management (TQM) programme was instituted. A critical mass of Dowty Fuel Systems' senior executives were 'bought in' to the TQM process from the outset, following an off-site awareness day run by Peratec Consultants. From this group, a steering committee was set up and many TQM executive techniques were put into practice. One of the first was analysis of the cost of quality (COQ). This is the measure of the cost of conformance – deliberate investment made to ensure good quality – weighed against the cost of getting it wrong. A £50 million business, Dowty discovered that £6 million was being lost through non-conformance: this was a conservative estimate.

Just 4 weeks after analysing COQ, Dowty put corrective action teams (CATs) in place to determine key processes and methods for improvement, and implement performance measures. This swift action was a vital part of the plan to gain quick results.

Each CAT was set a major objective. A CAT in the machining department, for example, was required to halve errors in 6 months. The team met its target in the required 6 months; after 10 months they had achieved an 82% improvement. Other statistics are equally impressive. In 3 years, Dowty Fuel Systems has improved already healthy margins by 50% and trebled its return on capital. Service to customers has also improved considerably.

Source: 'Fuelling change', Voyager, British Midland In-Flight Magazine, *Mediamark, London,* **Sep./Oct.**, *p. 58, 1994*

The following elements are referred to directly or implied:

- Identify sources of non-conformance.
- Process performance data.
- Use of quality costs.
- Policy deployment.
- Performance measurement.
- Teamwork.
- Employee involvement.

Whilst some techniques from the first three categories are mentioned, the overall emphasis is on TQM, especially in the involvement of employees and teams. There is no direct reference to the involvement of suppliers or customers, though service to customers is clearly an important concern.

The total quality approach requires considerable organization-wide support, and is effectively an overall organizational change process. Bessant et al. (1994, pp. 12–13) have argued that 'partial TQM' has been unsuccessful in many organizations because there has not been the recognition or commitment to change, resulting in the need to relaunch the TQM effort. Quoting a survey by A. T. Kearney, Bessant et al identify the following factors are identified as relevant to successful TQM efforts:

- *Performance measurement*: successful firms were twice as likely to measure key parameters and to benchmark the competition.
- *Focus on customers*: often extending to involvement of customers in the improvement programmes.
- *Changing behaviour/culture management programmes*: such as cross-functional teams and employee empowerment programmes.

They go on to identify the following propositions which it is suggested are critical to the success of total quality relationships in the supply chain:

- The need for co-ordination mechanisms in the relationship.
- Recognition of a shared relationship.
- Clear strategy for total quality in the relationship.
- Clear mandate in support of the shared strategy from senior management.
- Supportive internal relationships within the customer and supplier organizations.
- A clear process for continuous improvement.
- An emerging structure for the relationship itself, represented by joint teams with their own resources and developing culture.

INVESTIGATE

- *What approach does your organization use to assess supplier quality? What aspects of quality are considered, and what tools and techniques are used? Have you attempted to implement a TQM approach and, if so, are the success factors identified by Bessant et al. present?*

Delivery

Costs of delivery shortfall include production hold-ups, delays in supplying customers, additional effort devoted to chasing up supplies and, ultimately, incurring penalties for late delivery. Delivery improvements may be achieved through examining transport routing, delivery quantity and frequency and inventory levels and locations at customer and supplier.

The interrelationships between these aspects of delivery performance are recognized in a comprehensive approach, such as just-in-time. Hines (1994, pp. 44–48) outlines the guiding principles of a just-in-time (JIT) delivery process as follows:

- *Just-in-time*: producing finished goods just in time to deliver them, producing the semifinished goods just in time for assembly and resupplying with purchased parts just in time to use them.
- *Stockless production*: from a well-buffered situation (with as much inventory as is needed to cover problems) to an unbuffered situation (with as much inventory as is needed to identify problems).
- *Preventing waste*: the minimum of materials, parts, space and work time that are necessary for the adding of value to products.
- *Flow production*: manufacturing as a flow without interruptions with raw materials moving through to a finished product without unnecessary handling or waiting time.
- *Pull system*: a movement from a situation where production determines the flow of materials to one in which the flow of materials determines production.
- *Dynamic responsibility*: a movement from static functional or machine-type based responsibility to a dynamic responsibility based on the needs of material flow.

Hines argues that such a comprehensive JIT system eliminates waste in inspection, transport, storage and set-up, resulting in reduced inventories, lead times, bottlenecks and quality problems, hence facilitating a more effective flow to the customer.

Discussion of the above improvement areas of quality, cost and delivery has presented models of best practice, largely based upon Japanese experience. You will no doubt be able to judge how applicable these approaches are to your own situation. At the very least, they should provide a standard to which any organization may aspire, in part if not in total. In the next section, methods of establishing and monitoring supplier performance will be examined which are perhaps more applicable to the less than ideal context in which most purchasers will find themselves.

Methods of establishing and monitoring supplier performance

Quality standards

The BS 5750 series sets out minimum general standards covering functions and facilities which establish, document and maintain an effective and economic quality system. The British Standards have been incorporated in European (EN 29000 to 29004) and International Standards (ISO 9000 to 9004). As a precursor to, or part of, a customer's supplier quality appraisal system, suppliers may be required to have achieved these general quality standards. However, for suppliers of critical components in manufacturing sectors, these minimum standards are insufficient to guarantee the necessary level of quality, and will need to be supplemented by more rigorous appraisal.

This is particularly the case as such quality awards have come under criticism, as the results of a survey outlined below indicate.

CIPS review of quality standards

The Chartered Institute of Purchasing and Supply has questioned a representative sample of its members about their experience of the quality standards such as BS 5750/ISO 9000 and EN 4500. The survey was undertaken at the request of the British Quality Foundation, which has established a Quality Infrastructure Task Force (QITF), following continuing adverse criticism in the media, and in industry generally, about the cost and complexity involved in obtaining registration.

Among areas identified as likely to require future examination were the implementation of standards for registration and accreditation, the registration of assessors and how they are used, the role of the DTI and the National Accreditation Council for Certification Bodies (NACCB) in formulating and implementing regulations, and the training of assessors and consultants.

Summary
BS 5750 is not working to best advantage. It is too expensive for smaller firms to seek certification.

There is too much paperwork involved. Some consultants are, in general, not professional enough or practical enough. The needs of most companies are not being adequately met.

Controls on consultants and certification bodies are not firm enough.

There is little common ground between assessment bodies.

BS 5750 is fine as a starter, but needs to build into a TQM system, properly controlled and managed.

Source: M. Gore, 'The quality infrastructure', Purchasing and Supply Management, **Feb.**, *41–43, 1994*

Whilst most of the above criticisms are procedural, and are common in any third-party assessment system, they do reinforce the need to adopt a wider concept of quality, and to apply additional methods of assuring supplier quality in respect of critical and high value supplies. Despite such criticisms, standards are being adopted by a rapidly increasing number of organizations, and continue to develop to take account of changing requirements. Developments to take into account environmental concerns are discussed in the extract presented below.

Quality and environmental standards

The main elements of the ultimate standard, which are already in place, are ISO 9000, BS 7750 as the likely model for a new green ISO standard, the EC Eco management and audit scheme regulation, and the health and safety regulations. On the drawing board, or already under way, are a new code of practice for procurement, which may become a BSI standard, a possible BS 8750 for the health and safety regulations, and the coming ISO 14000.

Where ISO 9000 (BS 5750) is customer or market-driven, BS 7750 is driven by these and also by strong legal and insurance motivations. This is because it is an ideal vehicle for both the health and safety regulations and the very important issues of product liability and public safety. Specifically, BS 7750 can be implemented to manage the traditional environmental issues, the health and safety of staff, public safety and product safety.

Where BS 5750 got a huge boost upon its adoption by ISO as the model for ISO 9000, and the ISO quality management standard in turn received the kick-start for its world-wide epidemic spread by the EC adopting it as EN 29000, the harmonized quality management standard for the Internal Market, BS 7750, has received an additional boost by the European Council of Ministers adopting the Eco management and audit scheme regulation, known as the Eco audit.

The central demand of the Eco audit is for an environmental management system, implemented to a standard such as BS 7750. This applies to a specified production site, and involves a 'systematic, periodic evaluation of environmental performance'. Everything else demanded by the audit, from formal stated policy to a programme of site measures and a management system, is more than catered for in BS 7750. One area of different emphasis, is that companies are expected to publish their environmental statements or results, while the BSI standard merely asks that the results be available to interested parties. Readers might like to know that environment award winning Yamanouchi has been making its results available for years, but no one comes in asking to see them.

The companies 'participating' (which means achieving) in the EC scheme can use an Eco audit logo and will be published in the official journal of the EC, a kind of honours list, or EC-wide register of members.

You can have a quality, ISO 9000 certified product, and manufacture it in an environmentally unfriendly, and even dangerous, way; it is very difficult, however, to provide a dirty and dangerous quality service. This means that it is much easier for services companies to implement one system which covers both elements.

Source: B. Rothery, 'ISO 9000 – What's next on the agenda?, Professional Purchasing, Trident Publishing, Dublin, pp. 24–27, June 1994

Vendor rating

Supplier performance will generally be monitored by some form of vendor rating which, as with vendor appraisal (see Chapter 3), may be carried out systematically, possibly through a computerized system, but could equally be a manual record maintained by individual purchasers on suppliers within their area of responsibility. Performance criteria to be monitored would normally include the following (Department of Trade and Industry, 1991, p. 14):

- *Quality*: defects, performance to specification, returns from customers.
- *Price*: changes, competitiveness.
- *Delivery*: on-time, correct quantity.
- *Administration*: errors on delivery notes or invoices.

Whilst quantitative measures for the above may be recorded, there are also more qualitative factors which should be taken into account, such as:

- After-sales service.
- Willingness to become involved in design, cost reduction, etc.
- Investment programmes.
- Good communication.
- Flexibility and proposing good ideas.
- Efficient paperwork.

These criteria may be weighted depending on their perceived importance, and each supplier scored against each criterion to produce an overall score.

It is important that you keep suppliers informed of their ratings. In addition to information on their own performance, you may wish to provide suppliers with league tables ranking suppliers showing their position, but not identifying other suppliers for reasons of confidentiality. You also need to hold regular meetings between buyers, users and suppliers to provide feedback on performance and to identify changes in order to bring about improvements. These should be discussed with the supplier and incorporated in supplier development programmes. Suppliers achieving particularly good results may be rewarded by a supplier award scheme, such as that operated by Dunlop Aviation.

Dunlop Aviation Division's supplier award scheme

Coventry-based Dunlop Aviation Division believes in giving credit where it's due. Through its new Supplier of the Year award, the aircraft component manufacturer sends a clear signal to suppliers that their performance affects its bottom line. Managing director Lou Fitzgerald says: 'At a time when the market is becoming increasingly competitive, and customers are demanding reductions in unit price, and improvements in quality and delivery performance, the manufacturer needs support from key suppliers in order to achieve these goals.'

The first such award, in 1987, went to California-based International Light Metals Corporation which had been supplying forgings for more than 10 years. The 1988 award went to Spencer Clark of Rotherham, the steels and alloys supplier judged Aviation Division's top performer on service and delivery, quality and reliability, cost control and flexibility of response to new requirements. And in 1989, another USA company Unirex Corporation of America collected its award for its excellent service as a stockholder in supplying fasteners.

'When we introduced these awards we hoped they would raise the profile of Aviation Division and give our suppliers something to strive for', says purchasing manager Laurence Burgess. 'We haven't been disappointed on either score. All three suppliers who've won the Supplier of the Year Award have seen it as a big morale boost. Unirex has its plaque hanging proudly in its main foyer. We see it as a way of recording excellence.'

Source: Department of Trade and Industry, Getting the Best from your Suppliers, Managing in the '90s, HMSO, London, p. 21, 1991

Quality awards

A number of quality awards, such as the Deming Award in Japan, the Baldridge Award in the USA, and the European Quality Award of the European Foundation for Quality Development provide recognition of organizations which have achieved not just the minimum standards represented by BS 5750 or ISO 9000, but have attained a level of excellence. The Baldridge Award is based on the following criteria (American Society for Quality Control, 1993):

- Senior Executive leadership.
- Information and analysis.
- Strategic quality planning.
- Human resource development and management.
- Management of process quality.
- Quality and operational results, measured by:
  - product and service quality
  - productivity improvement
  - waste reduction/elimination
  - supplier quality.
- Customer focus and satisfaction, assessed by:
  - customer satisfaction
  - customer satisfaction relative to competitors
  - customer retention
  - market share gain.

The Award criteria reflect the importance of quality as a total business solution, and as extending beyond the organization to both customers and suppliers within the supply chain.

INVESTIGATE

- *Which of the above methods does your organization use for establishing and monitoring supplier performance? If there are some which are not used, should you consider introducing them?*

Methods of improving performance

Getting close to your suppliers

A comprehensive and practical series of steps aimed at getting the best out of your suppliers, based upon developing a close relationship, are set out in the

Department of Trade and Industry's (DTI's) booklet *Getting the Best from your Suppliers* (1991, p. 14). These include the following:

- Share your business plans.
- Share your purchasing and supply plans.
- Encourage participation between users and operational staff at your suppliers.
- Use fun and games activities to improve communications with suppliers, such as prizes, supplier newsletters, and supplier open days.
- Improve information flows.

Rolls Royce hold annual Supplier Conferences at which there are presentations on market prospects, customer requirements, purchasing targets and supplier performance, and initiatives such as electronic data interchange (EDI). These provide a valuable opportunity to provide suppliers with information and to obtain feedback, but also to foster a sense of shared objectives in terms of meeting customer needs.

Relationship assessment

The Glasgow University based Supply Chain Management Group have developed a comprehensive methodology for assessing the effectiveness of the supply chain relationship between buying and supplying organizations. Criteria and measures for assessing the overall business relationship have been developed, including the following categories relating to supplier capability:

- *Company profile and strategy*: number of customers, per cent of sales taken by major companies, organization structure, financial health, certification, and market flexibility.
- *People*: skills, organization structure, autonomy and involvement of staff, training, flexibility, reward system, and attitudes towards joint action with customers.
- *Process*: design, plant capability, plant capacity, systems, process range, flexibility, and lead times.

When combined with other factors, this approach provides a mechanism for assessing not only a supplier's capability, but also the overall strengths and weaknesses of the customer–supplier relationship.

Supplier associations

This is a structured approach to improving communications with suppliers. Hines (1994, pp. 273–288) sees the supplier association as a new route to creating world class suppliers. It comprises the following sequential stages:

Preplanning
1 Benchmark present competitive position.
2 Select appropriate co-ordination and development tools.
3 Gain internal acceptance and create cross-functional team.
4 Select appropriate suppliers.

Planning
5 Benchmark supplier position.
6 Jointly target improvements.
7 Focus co-ordination and development activities.

Do
8 Undertake group activities.

Check
9 Measure improvements.

Act
10 Refocus size of group and target areas.

Once the whole process has been completed, there should be a loop back to Stage 5 and a reiteration of the cycle.

Supplier development

This is usually associated with action on the part of a major customer, such as Nissan in the case study below, to improve some aspect of the performance of its suppliers. Large companies can afford to invest in supplier development teams, involving engineering, design, production, quality and purchasing staff, who visit suppliers to analyse their production and logistics processes and suggest improvements. These are generally on a small scale individually, such as changing the layout of a workshop to reduce the time and duplication of effort in the production of a part. However, these small improvements can add up to produce considerable savings in time, better productivity and better quality. What aspects of Nissan's supplier development programme strike you as being of particular interest? You may wish to review the findings of Lamming's report (Lamming, 1994) on relations between UK vehicle manufacturers and their suppliers presented in Chapter 5 before reading this extract.

Nissan's supplier development programme

Nissan has its own approach for evaluating potential suppliers and for setting, measuring and monitoring on-going improvements. The system is known as CESES (Common European Supplier Evaluation System). This evaluates performance against quality, cost, delivery, development and management. A distillation of everything Nissan has learned since 1985, it provides a mechanism for defining requirements, measuring a supplier's performance and capability, and providing regular feedback. Clinical and intrusive it may sound, but suppliers welcome it.

Ivor Vaughan, chairman and chief executive of Leicestershire-based Rearsby Automotive, has supplied Nissan with gear shifts and hand brakes since 1986:

> 'Back in the early '80s, I recognized that the only way we could accelerate our performance on delivery, cost, quality and customer support was to keep pace with the front runners – and the world class players were Japanese.
>
> I told my workforce that Nissan would drag us kicking and screaming into world class – or put us out of business. When Nissan told us the place was a mess, and we had to improve quality and training, I was ready for it. I love the feedback. It's three-monthly, it's accurate and it tells us how Nissan colleagues see us.
>
> I may not always like what Nissan tells me. It's a very demanding customer – but we address the problems together and I find that very stimulating.
>
> There's a lot said about partnership, but Nissan *lives* it. I am always referred to as the supplier. Nissan makes the commitment and its actions support it.'

The car company's commitment to help suppliers improve their performance is far from cosmetic. In 1988, it launched its Supplier Development Team (SDT) programme so its specialists could work with suppliers to make the kaizen concept a reality. Suppliers' cross-functional teams, trained and supported by Nissan engineers, are charged with making measurable improvements in specific manufacturing areas in a maximum of ten days.

To date, over 60 suppliers have participated in the full-blown SDT programme. Ivor Vaughan again: 'Prior to the Micra launch, our assembly time for the gear shift was 2.9 minutes. After a joint team had looked at the operation, the time was cut to 0.9 minutes. We have since done a joint kaizen exercise with Rover, sharing what we've learned from Nissan.'

At Britax (Wingard), managing director John Churchill has gone one stage further, taking the SDT model to his own 45-strong supplier base. Based in Porchester, near Portsmouth, Britax (Wingard) designs and makes car mirrors. Says Churchill:

> 'Nissan believes in, and practises, true partnership. It is fair and reasonable and very supportive. When we delivered products that were not up to standard, it helped us make improvements, monitored the programmes and, once everything was okay, forgot the incident. That cements a relationship.
>
> As for our own SDT programme, we have 26 teams and we've made tremendous strides in increasing productivity and redu-

cing costs. We also have our own SDT expert helping our suppliers apply the principles. And we share our five-year plan with our suppliers.'

For its part, Nissan is also working on 'sending ripples of improvement' down the supplier chain. Peter Hill explains:

'We looked to see how far the concept of partnership was being applied in the supply chain. Currently, it's not very far. So we've set up two-day workshops to introduce purchasing people from our suppliers to techniques that they in turn can pass down the chain. Forty suppliers have done the programme so far.'

Although Nissan is creating a blueprint for partnership sourcing in the automotive industry, Peter Hill and Bob Hampson, general manager purchasing liaison for Nissan (Europe), are the first to admit there's a long way to go. A recent initiative aims to move the company and its suppliers to 'a new level of achievement' in 1996, by setting best practice targets and measuring improvements in the five CESES categories. Says Bob Hampson:

'Our internal target is to get a totally open relationship with all our suppliers. But we don't believe we'll get to that stage with even 90 per cent of our current suppliers until 1996 – that's over ten years after we started in 1985. It's a process that requires time and effort. It means doing what you say you'll do and not walking away when times are tough.'

Hill believes it is critical that suppliers are convinced that baring their souls will not lead to a customer taking advantage. 'If a supplier takes an open book approach so you can crawl all over his factory and then you start squeezing margins, you'll destroy any trust that's been built up over the years.'

Neither Nissan nor its suppliers pretend the partnership is easy. The trick, says Hill, is to solve the problems together. Adds Hampson:

'When you talk about partnership and improvement, people tend to think about putting bad things right. To a certain extent that is what we've been doing. But the real benefits of partnership come when you jointly agree where you need to be in future, matching business objectives and enabling forward planning and investment decisions to be made on a mutually-beneficial basis.'

Source: R. Rees, 'No flexing of powerful muscles', in DTI Boardroom Report: Best Practice in Purchasing, *Findlay Publications, Horton Kirby, pp. 32–34, 1993*

The Nissan case provides evidence in relation to a number of issues raised in Lamming's report and earlier in this chapter. First, the suppliers interviewed seem genuinely appreciative of Nissan's assistance, and emphasize the mutual trust on which supplier development is based. This suggests that Nissan is not typical of the UK vehicle manufacturers surveyed in Lamming's report, which found that where supplier development is practised there is often a sense of dogma and domination of suppliers by more powerful customers. Secondly, both Nissan and the suppliers in the SDP recognize the importance of spreading best practice back down the supply chain. This recognizes the need identified in Lamming's report for vehicle manufacturers to make effective use of the technical abilities of components suppliers, and for raw materials suppliers to adopt lean supply practices. Thirdly, it seems surprising that Nissan do not object to the benefits of the supplier development programme being passed on to a major competitor, Rover. However, as it is more than likely that suppliers will learn new ways of improving their performance through adapting to other customers' requirements, there is a clear opportunity for all parties to benefit, especially the end customer who will eventually purchase better quality cars at lower relative cost. Finally, the specific case of the reduction in the time taken to assemble a gear shift from 2.9 to 0.9 minutes affords a striking illustration of the practical benefits of supplier development. With such radical improvements available, it is not surprising that most western manufacturers are seeking to replicate the mainly Japanese practices outlined earlier in this chapter.

You do not, however, have to be a powerful customer to gain the benefits of supplier development. As a result of working closely with your suppliers of critical goods or services, you can identify areas where improvements can be made on a joint basis, whether in terms of reducing costs, improving quality or delivery.

Summary

This chapter has identified areas where improvements may be made in supplier performance, in particular in cost, quality and delivery. Ways of establishing and monitoring supplier performance have been examined, including the use of standards, quality awards, vendor rating and supplier awards. Finally, ways of improving supplier performance have been presented, in particular by adopting an open and collaborative approach involving activities such as supplier open days, supplier associations, relationship assessment and supplier development. Ideally, you and your suppliers will recognize a mutual benefit in seeking to improve performance, and it will not be one way: you and your colleagues in other departments will also need to be open to suggestions for change from your suppliers.

With this chapter we end this section of the book on sourcing, in which we have explored broad strategic approaches to analysing and managing the

supply chain in general and developing relationships with individual suppliers. In the next section, on contracting, we look at processes at the more
operational level, involving planning and specifying requirements, selecting
suppliers and establishing contracts for supply. These areas are, however,
not distinct, but need to be closely interrelated: without the former, there can
be no assurance that you are buying in favourable markets from suitable
suppliers with whom you may wish to develop mutually beneficial business
relationships. Without proper attention to the latter, all your market research
and analysis of suppliers may be undone by incorrect specification, selection
of suppliers which is unethical, discriminatory or does not ensure competitive supplies, or insufficient attention given to contracts resulting in disad-
vantageous terms and conditions or failure to supply. Thus, whilst the
division between sourcing and contracting derives from a logical approach,
the reality is that these processes interact continually, and you may find
yourself carrying them out at the same time almost without noticing. But
it is important that you pay adequate attention to both sets of processes,
either individually or as part of a buying team or purchasing department, so
as to gain the maximum benefit for the organization from your buying
expertise.

Activities

1   Write a memo to your Purchasing Manager assessing your organization's approach to supplier quality and outlining how it may be
improved.

---

2   You have been asked to present a paper at your organization's annual
supplier conference, outlining various approaches to developing closer
supplier relations, in particular supplier associations, relationship
assessment and supplier development. Identify the costs and benefits
of introducing such approaches for both your organization and your
suppliers, and present a plan for introducing whichever methods you
think appropriate to your organization.

References and further reading

American Society for Quality Control (1993) *The Malcolm Baldridge National Quality Award*,
   ASQC, Milwaukee, WI
Bell, D., McBride, P. and Wilson, G. (1994) *Managing Quality*, Butterworth-Heinemann, Oxford
Bessant, J., Levy, P., Sang, R. and Lamming, R. (1994) 'Managing successful total quality relation-
   ships in the supply chain', *European Journal of Purchasing and Supply Management*, **1** (1)

British Standards Institution (1990) *BS 6143: Part 2 Guide to the Economics of Quality*, BSI, Milton Keynes

Dale, B. D. (ed) (1994) *Managing Quality*, Prentice Hall International, Hemel Hempstead

Department of Trade and Industry (1991) *Getting the Best from your Suppliers*, HMSO, London

Hines, P. (1994) *Creating World Class Suppliers: Unlocking Mutual Competitive Advantage*, Financial Times/Pitman, London

Macbeth, D. K. and Ferguson, N. (1994) *Partnership Sourcing: An Integrated Supply Chain Approach*, Financial Times/Pitman, London

Syson, R. (1992) *Improving Purchase Performance*, Pitman, London

PART THREE

Contracting

7 Planning and specifying supply requirements

Introduction

In Part Two, we covered important aspects of the process of sourcing suppliers. Thus we have examined:

- The supply markets in which you are buying.
- The suppliers with which you wish to do business.
- Those with which you wish to develop longer term, partnership relationships for strategic supply.
- How the performance of your suppliers, and of the overall business relationship between your organization and your suppliers, may be improved.

With this chapter we start to examine the process of contracting, by which you obtain the particular products and services required by your organization. In doing so, you will draw on the knowledge of markets and suppliers developed in the sourcing process. You may draw upon those markets and suppliers for many individual contracts for a wide range of products and services over a number of years. Logically, contracting is seen as the subordinate process, taking place within the context established by sourcing. But you will also contribute to changes in markets and suppliers through the experience of each separate contracting process. Thus sourcing and contracting are not separate but linked processes, with constant feedback from one to the other.

The objectives of this chapter are to:

- Examine the planning of purchasing requirements.
- Explore the make/do or buy decision.
- Investigate the purpose and methods of specifications.
- Examine the process of contracting for services.
- Identify options for the agreement to supply.

Planning purchasing requirements

All organizations need to plan. Most will have strategic or corporate plans, which provide a direction for the organization and its staff. Identification of requirements is clearly of strategic importance, especially where key purchases are critical to the liquidity of a company or the performance of a new product. Examples are the timing, frequency and volume of aircraft purchases by major airlines and of critical components to a new model by an automobile manufacturer. In such cases purchases are planned up to 10 years in advance, and are obviously of critical importance to the organization's survival.

The various functions within the organization also need to develop their plans and ensure that they are integrated with organizational strategies. These could cover finance, investment, new product development, production, personnel, marketing, sales, etc. If you are responsible for the purchasing plan, you therefore need to ensure that it is related to organizational strategies (see Box 7.1), and is consistent with those of other relevant functions, in particular marketing, production and finance. For manufacturing processes, master schedules may be produced by engineering teams setting out the purchasing requirements, time-scales and delivery instructions, leaving little scope for purchasing initiative. However, in many organizations an integrated approach may be achieved through interdepartmental planning teams, in which purchasing plays a key role in advising on how various sourcing and contracting options may assist in achieving financial, marketing and production targets.

Purchasing could contribute to any or all of the following:

- Make/do or buy strategies, based upon analysis of the comparative costs and technical capabilities of in-house production or service performance against outside suppliers or contractors.
- Cost-reduction initiatives, by identifying alternative sources for high cost purchases; or by better specification; or through supplier development; or improved inventory and delivery strategies.
- New product development or market entry decisions based upon knowledge of suppliers of key components in suitable locations, and advice on timing of purchases.

As Box 7.1 suggests, we need to ensure that detailed purchasing plans cascade down from previous strategic decisions. They could include:

- Schedule of purchases of goods and services, with quantities required, lead times required to ensure delivery at the correct times and locations.
- Contracts requiring renewal or renegotiation, with lead times necessary to comply with organizational or legislative requirements.

Box 7.1 *Business and purchasing and supply objectives*

Business objectives	**Purchasing and supply objectives**
A statement of the position the firm is aiming for in its markets, including market share	The objective of providing the quantity and quality of supplies required by the market share and market positioning objectives
A key objective of, say, moving out of speciality markets and entering volume markets	A key objective of developing new, larger, suppliers and materials flow systems more geared to larger numbers of fewer parts whilst keeping total inventory volume low
A key objective to build new businesses which will generate positive cashflow as well as reasonable profits	Contribute to cashflow improvement through lower average inventory and by negotiating smaller delivery lots and/or longer payment terms
A plan to develop some specific new products or services	A plan to develop appropriate suppliers
An overall production/capacity plan, including an overall policy on make or buy	A plan to develop systems which integrate capacity planning and purchase planning, together with the policy on make or buy
A plan to introduce a cost-reduction programme	A plan to introduce supplies standardization and supplier reduction programmes
A financial plan, setting out in broad terms how the proposed capital expenditure is to be financed, together with an outline time-scale and an order in which the objectives need to be achieved	A financial plan, setting out broadly the profit contribution expected from purchasing and supply, together with the time in which it should be achieved and the priorities of the objectives

Source: Department of Trade and Industry, Building a Purchasing Strategy, Managing in the 90s, *HSMO, London, p. 6, 1993*

In planning the volume and timing of orders you need to take into account the organization's financial strategies and position, such as liquidity, planned investment and possible tax benefits of re-equipping at specific times. There may also be fixed budgets and annual accounting requirements, particularly in the public sector, which limit the opportunities for long-term planning of purchase requirements.

Any special purchasing initiatives, such as rationalization of the supply base, supplier development, inventory reduction or implementing electronic systems, may also be included to allow a complete overview of the workload.

You should revise your plans annually, but they may form part of rolling 3- or 5-year plans which would accommodate long-term projects, such as developing a new product or completing a major construction project. They may also be broken down into quarterly or monthly periods for monitoring purposes. This then provides the basis for you or your manager to allocate work to buying teams and individual buyers. Your plans may also incorporate savings and other targets, and mechanisms for monitoring and evaluating purchasing performance (see Chapter 10).

The following examples illustrate the different planning time-scales for buyers of steel pipe and packaging, respectively.

Buying steel pipe at British Gas

For steel pipe, we look 5 years ahead, asking what is the available capacity and demand. We hold meetings with customers from the regions to identify their needs. Whilst most of our business is with British Steel, we looked at manufacturers on the continent who can meet the specifications, and visit their steel plants.

On a quarterly basis, we ascertain requirements 6 months ahead, notify British Steel, obtain a detailed production plan for each week, analyse it to see if it meets the requirements. Then we raise purchase orders, monitor and track their production progress using a computer-based system to make sure quality specifications and deadlines are met.

Source: Interviews, Supplies and Contracts Officers, British Gas

---

Buying packaging at Nestlé Rowntree

Each of us is responsible for a type of packaging: tin, outer carton, foam, case, etc. I am responsible for cartons. I have to ensure the supply of packaging materials to enable continuous production. There are two ways of ordering:

1 Weekly planning sheets: to plan how many packages are required up to so many weeks ahead. We let the factory get down to 14 weeks of stock, then reorder, as it can take up to 10 weeks to supply. We must cover the production plan for all the factories.
2 Material ordering estimates: this covers anything seasonal or it could be a promotion. There may be up to 80 different cartons for Christmas products. For seasonal or promotional packs we are told how much to order. Marketing tells the planners how much we can sell.

Source: Interview, Purchasing Assistant, Nestlé Rowntree

INVESTIGATE

● *Do you know what the current purchasing plans and objectives and timescales of your organization are? How do they relate to the organization's strategic objectives? How can you contribute to their achievement through your own work?*

Make/do or buy

This is perhaps the most critical strategic decision for all organizations at present. Increasingly, private sector companies, both manufacturing and service, and public sector organizations are realizing that producing all the goods and services required by the organization themselves is not necessarily the most efficient and effective method. The following examples illustrate the make/do or buy decision in respect of a new product, the production of a new car model, and a new service, the introduction of vehicle inspection tests.

Make/do or buy: a new car model

Each vehicle part, how and by whom they will be assembled, as well as functions such as research, design, testing and advertising, could be subjected to the make/do or buy question. Thus parts may be manufactured by second- or third-tier suppliers, assembled by first-tier suppliers into packages such as complete seating assemblies and delivered to the main manufacturer. Research and design may be carried out in conjunction with suppliers and university research centres; major components and prototype models may be tested at other manufacturers' facilities or private test circuits; and advertising will be contracted out to an agency.

Do or buy: vehicle testing

The Department of Transport had to decide whether vehicle testing was a core function of high political significance in which ministers had a direct interest. This was not the case, and so in Britain vehicle testing was contracted out to private garages. However, in Northern Ireland it is carried out by an Agency of the Department of Environment, indicating that the context in which

> the do or buy decision is taken can make a difference to the out-
> come.

In addition to new products or services, organizations may wish to review periodically, or on a regular basis, all activities in order to determine whether they should be carried out in-house or contracted out. This is particularly the case in the public sector at present, where systematic time-tables for the competitive tendering of service contracts have been established, annual targets for which have been increased since the re-election of the Conservative government under John Major in April 1992. Thus an increasing proportion of public purchasers' time and expertise will be devoted to advising on and carrying out 'market testing' to establish whether a service can be provided more efficiently and effectively by a private sector contractor rather than the in-house team. Whilst you may not be responsible for strategic make/do or buy decisions, you will certainly be expected to contribute to the specification of the product or service, and through analysis of the supply market, supplier appraisal and selection of a suitable contractor.

Figure 7.1 shows a plan for the review of services provided by a government department or an executive agency. Whilst the option of contracting out the service directly to the private sector may be considered, most services are market tested, that is, the existing in-house staff are invited to submit a bid as well as private sector companies. Before the market testing process begins, it is important that the responsibilities of the client (the divisional manager who is responsible for letting and subsequently managing the contract) and contractor (the in-house staff currently delivering the service) need to be clearly distinguished so that potential outside providers are not at a disadvantage. The scope and nature of the service to be subjected to market testing is identified in the Statement of Requirement and Specification, in particular to determine whether the current level of service and costs are appropriate to future requirements. Once the specification has been established, in-house and external bids are invited, and evaluated against pre-established criteria. If the contract is awarded in-house, then efficiency measures identified in the bid are implemented so that the service may be provided at the tender price. Alternatively, the outside contractor may take on responsibility for some or all of the in-house staff. Performance and cost are monitored and reviewed prior to putting the service out to tender again at the end of the contract period.

Whilst such a systematic and structured approach is mandatory in most parts of the public sector, private sector organizations which have not examined the products and services currently manufactured or provided in-house may benefit from adopting a similar approach. Arguments for and against contracting out are outlined below.

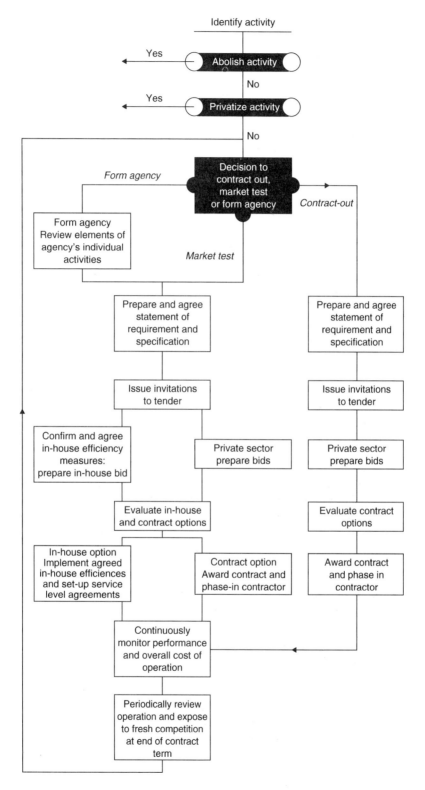

Figure 7.1 The market-testing process. (From the Office of Public Service and Science, *The Governments Guide to Market Testing*, HMSO, London, 1993, p. 6)

Arguments for contracting out

- Enables the organization to concentrate on its core activities where its expertise is greatest.
- Takes advantage of the technical and business expertise of suppliers for whom the product or service is its main business.
- Should reduce costs in staff and other resources directly employed on the product or service as well as overheads.
- Should increase quality, as the contractor has greater expertise.
- Should reduce the range of products directly purchased to support in-house production or performance of the service.
- Allows greater flexibility in terms of additional production capacity when required without high fixed investment costs in new plant.
- Clearer specification of the product or service required.
- Provides a route to world class performance where your contractors are innovative and have unique expertise or products.

Arguments against contracting out

- The costs of the market-testing process in terms of identifying, assessing and selecting potential contractors, particularly in the public sector where prescribed tendering procedures have to be followed.
- Increased responsibility for monitoring and managing contractors.
- Increased risk of supply failure or poor quality if the wrong contractor is selected.
- Employees may be affected by uncertainty, with some job losses and lowering of employment conditions for those retained or taken on by the contractor.

What arguments for and against contracting out can you identify in the following extract?

Make or buy at IBM

The shift in balance from 'make' to 'buy' needs a different level of experience, . . . The emphasis on providing solutions to our customers means that we have to react fast. Product development cycles used to be five years. Last year it was down to 18 months. In two years time it could be just one year. We must have those first few months with the right product on the market to meet the early demand and maximize profit.

Our suppliers have to react as fast as we do. We're constantly looking at new suppliers. We need niche technology leaders. At IBM today, 'make or buy?' decisions are more often the latter. At first I thought that this was because we just couldn't cover the ground in the time available. But I soon realized that the dedication of some organizations means that they are more expert . . .

We are investigating using outside purchasing and management expertise for certain functions. We want one company to manage all our building and office services here at Portsmouth – from cutting the grass to running the cafeteria. We will buy a level of service at a price.

Gillett believes the same ideas can be applied to electronics purchasing. At present IBM spends £500 million a year on electronic components alone (excluding internal purchases). It has 300 'preferred' suppliers of electronic and electromechanical components and software. Although these are predominantly component manufacturers, the list also includes contract manufacturers and distributors.

These 300 suppliers cover about 80% of our manufacturing needs in Havant and Greenock. The problem is that there is a tail of about 3000 suppliers accounting for the other 20% . . .

For IBM, make or buy decisions depend on a number of factors.

If there is a very large up front investment needed and there are acknowledged specialists already established then we will usually buy in. If the component is technology critical and/or liable to erratic supply, then we will make it ourselves.

However, this route is not always plain sailing as IBM found out with the risc processor used in its workstations. Gillett would not deny that IBM was late into the workstation market. However, he said: 'If you have technology leadership, as we have with our risc processor, you can still be successful coming in late to a maturing market . . . '.

Subcontractors have to be flexible, to react to the ups and downs of the market. They are responsible and accountable for dealing with their own suppliers. 'For many this is a dynamic new business. They are stretching themselves and management skills are particularly important.'

*Source: Extracts from an interview with John Gillett, IBM UK, Country Manager of Procurement, in L. Joselyn, 'Procurement task requires a new way of thinking', New Electronics, **Jan.**, 50–52, 1991*

The main advantages identified are:

- To enable faster product development.
- Taking advantage of suppliers who are niche technology leaders.

- Making use of suppliers who have more expertise than IBM.
- To reduce the 'tail' of low value or volume suppliers.
- To reduce the range of products directly purchased.

Whilst no disadvantages are specifically identified, Gillett does emphasize the importance of retaining areas of work which are critical or subject to erratic supply, though the example of the risc processor shows that in-house production is not necessarily without its own risks!

INVESTIGATE

- *Does your organization have a make/do or buy strategy? What products and services are covered? In what ways are you involved in or affected by the outcome of make or buy decisions?*

The outcome of make/do or buy decisions will feed into the plans for purchasing, in that purchases for any product or service which is contracted out will normally become the responsibility of the contractor, as indicated by John Gillett. On the other hand, identifying and selecting a supplier for the product or service will become a purchasing responsibility, and there will be a much greater responsibility for monitoring and managing the contractor, especially if the contract covers a complete subassembly or a range of related services. The programme of products and services to be contracted out, together with the goods and services to support the organization's core functions, provides the total requirements which are to be purchased.

Specifications

It is essential that requirements are specified clearly in order to ensure that the product or service supplied is indeed what the organization requires. In many cases, specification can be relatively precise, and relate to products in everyday use. However, many can be extremely complex, especially for the supply of services, where detailed performance standards and monitoring need to be specified in service level agreements. Similarly, for technically complex products, specification of functional or performance requirements, rather than a detailed design alone, may result in innovative solutions, and save on expensive retooling by suppliers.

Burt (1989, p. 43) identifies the problems of unclearly stated requirements resulting in costly quality defects, and incorrectly defined specifications which, even should the product meet the specification, will not perform the task required. These problems are more likely to be present where changes in process, supplier or raw materials are involved.

Purchasing is clearly dependent on customers determining and communicating their requirements. Nevertheless, we should adopt a proactive approach by advising and assisting customers to make purchases of the required products and services to the correct specification through:

- Providing information on available products with analyses of their performance.
- Providing information on sources of supply and the extent to which they meet the organization's supplier appraisal criteria, such as quality, price, total cost, delivery, etc.
- Identifying risk factors related to particular products or suppliers, including technical, financial and political risks.
- Identifying opportunities for standardization or consolidation of requirements across departments and locations; this may be facilitated through a computerized purchasing system.

The needs of the customer are of course paramount, but you should not simply accept them. You should be ready to challenge customers' needs and desired performance levels if necessary. Requests for more expensive branded products with marginal, if any, performance benefits, should certainly be queried. In many organizations this requires the purchaser to challenge the professional expertise of specialist, and higher status staff, such as consultants in the National Health Service, but the overriding concern should be to ensure the most efficient and effective method of meeting the identified need.

Davies (1985) identifies constraints and limitations resulting from unchallenged specifications: limited competition if it is based on a specific item or equipment; specification of custom-built items when standard items are readily available; overengineered specifications, with performance requirements in excess of those actually essential.

You may also invite potential suppliers to discuss the design of complex products or services. This should ensure that potential suppliers are clear about the nature and purpose of the requirement, may provide innovative technical solutions, improve the quality, or reduce the cost of the product. The illustration from Ford's presented below indicates the advantages of early involvement of suppliers. However, there may be restrictions on such consultations in the public sector.

Early supplier involvement in design at Ford UK

Traditionally when product development released the drawing we would have sent out for three quotes and placed the business. Now we encourage the early involvement of suppliers. Why should the engineer work in isolation? In the new programme for aluminium cylinder blocks, we spoke to suppliers, nominated some to work with product development groups and engineering.

> We must involve the product development engineer, component suppliers, manufacturing engineer and machine tool manufacturers. There were maybe three or four possible suppliers of the aluminium cylinder block, but we decided to major on one or two of them. In the old days we worked separately, but we now have simultaneous engineering meetings to get the best ideas and reduce the length of development time.
>
> *Source: Interview, Procurement Planning Manager, Ford UK*

Methods of specifying requirements

There are three main types of specification, functional, performance and technical, identified by the Central Unit of Purchasing in a guidance note on *Specification Writing* (CUP, 1991). These are defined as follows (p. 15):

1   *Functional*: 'Define the purpose of the requirement. They define the task or desired result by focusing on what is to be achieved; they do not describe the method of achieving the intended result.'
2   *Performance*: 'Define the required performance parameters by setting out details of operating inputs and outputs; they do not state how this performance will be achieved.'
3   *Technical*: 'Define the limits of compatibility or to describe an item which has already been designed or has been prescribed.' Examples of technical specifications are physical characteristics, e.g. dimensions, strength, purity, toxicity levels; design details; material properties; processes, e.g. methods of manufacture; maintenance requirements; and operational requirements, e.g. equipment availability levels.'

CUP argues that nearly all requirements can be specified in functional and performance terms, and that technical specifications should be additional to these where greater detail or precision is necessary. However, these may limit the scope for suppliers to provide innovative or alternative solutions.

The effects of using technical and functional specifications for the supply of a boiler are illustrated in Box 7.2.

Whilst this example shows clearly the benefits of using functional specifications, in many cases it is essential to provide additional technical information to communicate your needs fully to suppliers. Increasingly these may be expressed in terms of national and international standards. Those most commonly used have been developed by the British Standards Institution (BSI), the European Committee for Standardization (CEN) and the International Standards Organization (ISO). Standards for electrical equipment have been developed by the International Electro-technical Commission (IEC) and the European Committee for Electro-technical Standardization (CENELEC).

Box 7.2 *Technical versus functional specifications*

In the case of a **technical approach**, the requirements are laid down in technical descriptions or technical specifications. The seller will be obliged to deliver precisely according to these technical specifications. The measurable specifications will be examined on delivery and are a yardstick for judging whether the seller has met his obligations.

In the case of a **functional approach**, the requirements are defined functionally in the most general way possible. An attempt is made to describe the result of the delivery in such a way that the perceptible effects or yield for the user, or in other words the useful effects, are indicated. One takes as a basis the operational function which the goods bought must fulfil. The value of the goods delivered is tested according to the extent to which it fulils the requirement or function to be met, not on the basis of what the goods actually deliver but which is not required.

Example

I buy a central-heating boiler for my house which can heat the house up to 22°C. The tender demand could take the following form:

Technical specifications: 50 kW, gas-fired
Functional specifications: a boiler which can heat my house up to 22°C with a minimum outside
                             temperature of −30°C

Effects of the two approaches:

Technically specified	*Functionally specified*
The supplier has no alternative. Should a 50 kW boiler be beyond his range of products, he cannot deliver	The supplier can look for the boiler within his range of products which can deliver this performance
Only one type of boiler is considered	The supplier can submit alternative offers classified according to: – fuel – technical system. Even alternative solutions can be considered
Result: If the supplier meets his obligations, the boiler installed will deliver 50 kW. Therefore the temperature in the house is not relevant for the supplier	*Result:* If the supplier meets his obligation, it will be possible to warm the house up to 22°C

Buying on the basis of technical specifications

Advantages:
- Offers can be expected which are deliverable and have demonstrated their worth in the past
- One knows precisely what one is getting and can verify this exactly at a later stage

Disadvantages:
- Possibility of there being few tenderers
- The specifications can discriminate in favour of a certain supplier, which can be commercially less desirable
- The buyer takes personal responsibility for the correctness of the specifications
- Products are bought which must function under conditions with respect to which they have never demonstrated their worth

Buying on the basis of functional specifications

Advantages:
- The seller is responsible for the equipment delivering the result and return which the buyer had in mind on concluding the sale
- The inventiveness of the tenderers is stimulated – the functional approach can, through competition, stimulate the development of well-founded solutions which are more advantageous in terms of purchase or operating costs
- With respect to the final interpretation of the function, more responsibility lies with the seller

- The drawing up of the specifications does not automatically have to be carried out by a (technical) specialist who knows all there is to know about product specifications

Disadvantages:
- The drawing up of the functional requirements demands initiative in accordance with policy
- The diversity of offers makes the choice more difficult. Therefore, on evaluating the tender there is more calculation work
- The buyer will have to examine the product from the seller carefully in order to determine whether, apart from the functionality itself, there are any additional objections to the way in which the seller realizes the functionality

Source: Extracts from: J. A. M. van Noord, Contracting on the basis of Functionality, *Irish Institute of European Affairs, Leuven, March 1993*

These standards define products by a combination of their dimensions, performance, design or safety requirements. Standards therefore provide a common basis for communicating your detailed requirements to suppliers. The advantages of standardization identified by Lysons (1993, p. 108) are listed below:

- Removal of uncertainty as to what is required.
- Saving time and money in preparing company specifications and correspondence to clarify requirements.
- Accurate comparison of quotations.
- Reduction in error and conflict.
- Saving in inventory and cost through variety reduction.
- Reduced investment in spares for capital equipment.
- Reduced cost of material handling, e.g. use of pallets.
- Elimination of the need to buy by brand name.
- Irregular purchases of non-standard equipment are highlighted.

However, you should ensure that the standards specified are not too stringent for the function which the product is required to perform, and do not restrict competition either between suppliers or from other countries.

Some of the other methods of technical specification identified by Lysons (1993, pp. 109–111) are discussed below:

- *Brand or trade name*: Users may express a preference for a branded product, and this method avoids the need to produce a detailed specification. Against this, it may be an expensive method, there may only be a single supplier, and it would be illegal under the EC Public Procurement Directives.
- *Chemical analysis of physical characteristics*: This method may be essential where hazardous goods are involved. These may be tested by either supplier, buyer, or an independent organization such as the British Standards Institution or the National Measurement Accreditation Service.
- *Sample*: Lysons says this is a particularly good method in relation to printing, raw materials and products such as cloth. However, the

buyer cannot be certain the bulk will correspond exactly to the sample, although there is a legal responsibility on the supplier to ensure that this is the case.

- *Drawing*: A detailed drawing may be necessary for engineered products or buildings, though as the illustration from Ford's showed, close collaboration on such drawings with partnership suppliers will help to avoid unnecessary or expensive design features and may result in innovative solutions.

Service specifications

Detailed guidance on specifying services in the context of market testing and compulsory competitive tendering has been produced by various government bodies (see, in particular, Office of Public Service and Science, *The Government's Guide to Market Testing*, 1993).

The service specification provides the basis for:

- The contract.
- Enforcement of the contract.
- Monitoring of the contract.

The service specification defines what the purchaser or client wishes to buy, what the supplier or contractor should provide, and should be as explicit as possible in defining the tasks and standards to which the work should be done. It indicates:

- *What is being tendered*: in terms of the nature and scope of the service, e.g. grounds maintenance, vehicle maintenance, major works, cleaning, etc., grouped geographically or by value, single or multiple contracts.
- *Contract details*: i.e. type and duration of contract.
- *Responsibilities of the client*: holds budget; specifies work; determination of scheduled, unscheduled and emergency work; agreement of pricing schedules; monitoring of contract; provision of equipment and property; provision of energy services; approval of variations; payment of contractor.
- *Responsibilities of the contractor*: staffing of contract; health and safety procedures; pricing of work; provision of labour and materials; transport of labour and materials; working to agreed quality and time-scales; recording of labour and materials costs; seeking variations; invoicing client; making a profit.
- *Standards required*: how will quality be monitored? Outputs; frequencies; materials quality; resource quality; technical standards?
- *Profiles of locations*: addresses of locations; map or area plan; area dimensions; volumes; special requirements, e.g. annual cleaning.
- *Constraints*: holidays; access times; seasonal work; security arrangements; liaison with local client representatives; use of subcontractors.

- *Financial arrangements*: collection of money; documentation, e.g. timesheets; billing procedures; pricing reviews; pricing mechanism.
- *Bill of quantities*: schedule of parts, pricing schedule.
- *Penalty arrangements*: non-performance penalties; default notices; quality penalties; rectification notices; recording of penalty points; financial penalties.
- *Termination arrangements*: disputes; clearing of sites; termination of contract.

Figure 7.2 shows the role of the service specification in the market testing process in a government department. As we saw in Figure 7.1, the market-testing process starts with a review of the service currently being provided.

Service Review: to define exactly what service is currently provided and at what cost:

- Resources used: costs, staff numbers, skills, grades, equipment and services.
- Current performance: accounts, existing statistics or performance measures.
- Operation of existing services and future plans: reorganization, legislation or other changes.
- Changes in relationships and interfaces: with the department and other actors.

This is followed by benchmarking to establish standards which the service provider will be expected to achieve in the future.

Benchmarking: to establish the nature of the future service requirement:

- Critical success factors for service provision.
- Assist in creating a framework of aims, objectives, targets and performance indicators.
- Provide quality criteria.
- Establish critical failure issues.
- Initial costing to determine need for European Community (EC) and/ or General Agreement on Tariffs and Trade (GATT) advertisement.
- Detailed cost breakdown by functions and cost types against which tenders can be evaluated and the successful bidder monitored.

This then forms the basis for the specification, the content of which is outlined in Figure 7.2.

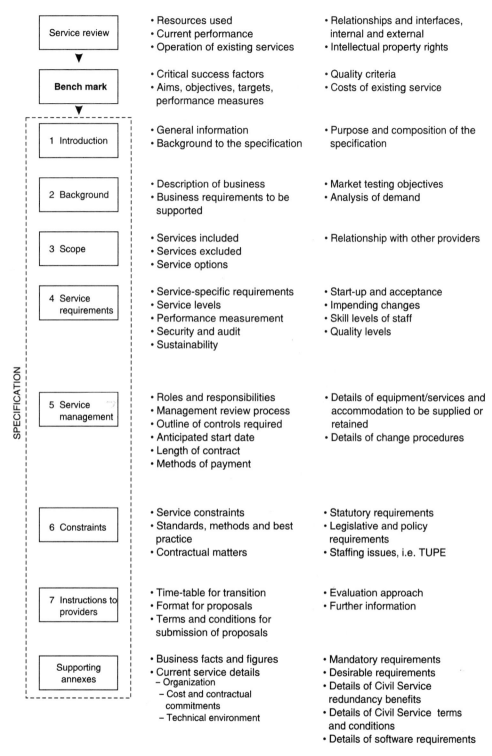

SPECIFICATION

Service review	• Resources used • Current performance • Operation of existing services	• Relationships and interfaces, internal and external • Intellectual property rights
Bench mark	• Critical success factors • Aims, objectives, targets, performance measures	• Quality criteria • Costs of existing service
1 Introduction	• General information • Background to the specification	• Purpose and composition of the specification
2 Background	• Description of business • Business requirements to be supported	• Market testing objectives • Analysis of demand
3 Scope	• Services included • Services excluded • Service options	• Relationship with other providers
4 Service requirements	• Service-specific requirements • Service levels • Performance measurement • Security and audit • Sustainability	• Start-up and acceptance • Impending changes • Skill levels of staff • Quality levels
5 Service management	• Roles and responsibilities • Management review process • Outline of controls required • Anticipated start date • Length of contract • Methods of payment	• Details of equipment/services and accommodation to be supplied or retained • Details of change procedures
6 Constraints	• Service constraints • Standards, methods and best practice • Contractual matters	• Statutory requirements • Legislative and policy requirements • Staffing issues, i.e. TUPE
7 Instructions to providers	• Time-table for transition • Format for proposals • Terms and conditions for submission of proposals	• Evaluation approach • Further information
Supporting annexes	• Business facts and figures • Current service details – Organization – Cost and contractual commitments – Technical environment	• Mandatory requirements • Desirable requirements • Details of Civil Service redundancy benefits • Details of Civil Service terms and conditions • Details of software requirements

Figure 7.2 Anatomy of a specification. (Adapted from Central Computer and Telecommunications Agency, *Producing a Statement of Service Requirements*, CCTA, London, 1993, 10)

The process of specification for a cleaning contract is outlined below.

Specifying a cleaning service

Specifications should detail all the objectives that are to be met in service contracts. They should also provide a yardstick by which to judge each competitive tender on an equal basis.

Unfortunately, few who have the responsibility for placing cleaning contracts, which may involve many thousands of pounds, have had any formal training in the drafting of specifications.

When going out to tender, three separate procedures are involved:

- The preparation of the cleaning specification.
- The drafting of the tender return documentation.
- The estimate of the manpower requirements and the evaluation of tenders.

It is important to remember that the preparation of the specification has a number of functions. It forms the basis of a contract between the client and the contractor, defines the minimum acceptable standards to be attained, details what cleaning processes need to be carried out, and dictates the frequencies with which they should be undertaken. It also specifies the areas to be cleaned and enables an accurate costing of the cleaning operation.

An effective specification provides a standard against which the quality of cleaning may be assessed, thereby allowing the implementation of suitable quality control or monitoring procedures. There are five separate components:

- The schedule of conditions which details the terms under which the contract is to be operated.
- The general notes which clarify operational aspects of the contract.
- The definition of cleaning terms providing a glossary of the terms used in the specification and detailing exactly what processes are involved, how they are achieved and what standards are sought.
- The schedule describing the accommodation to be cleaned, together with floor areas and floor types and classifying this accommodation according to usage.
- The cleaning schedules which specify the actual cleaning processes that are to be undertaken and the frequencies with which they are to be carried out.

Source: E. Brown, 'Preparation for the cleaning specification', Government Purchasing, **May,** *p. 20, 1994*

Options for service contracts

As we saw in Chapter 4, the way in which services are grouped together into contracts can have a significant impact upon the number and scope of service providers to be managed by the organization. This is only one factor in the judgement as to how, if at all, services might be combined. The options include:

- *Single service*: e.g. cleaning or catering.
- *Multiservice*: combines several services, e.g. cleaning (interior and exterior) together with laundry.
- *Group service*: involves linked groups, e.g. hotel or estate services:
  - Hotel: catering, portering, domestic, linen and laundry, security, residential accommodation, reception/switchboard.
  - Estates: works and maintenance, design, car parking, grounds maintenance, waste disposal, pest control and transport.
  Other possible group services include computer services, administration and finance.
- *Total site services/facilities management*: all non-core services for one or more sites using in-house or commercial contractor with responsibility to:
  - Develop multi-skilled work teams with flexibility between service elements run as integrated service.
  - Subletting part of contract to other expert contractors whilst retaining contractual responsibility.

You may wish to consider the following factors in the choice of service contract option:

- *Number of separate market-testing exercises and contracts to manage*: fewer means less administration, but may stretch contractors' capacity and client/purchaser manager's expertise.
- *Scope of contract*: multiservice, group service, etc., contracts.
  - May limit competition, as fewer contractors are capable of carrying out all the services specified
  - May exclude small and/or local contractors
  - May bias the contract in favour of an in-house bid.

However, early planning and advertising of plans will allow potential contractors to develop expertise and linkages with other potential contractors and thus enable the facilities management option to be considered.

Type and duration of supply agreement

In addition to the specification of the product or service required, it is important to ensure that the type and duration of the supply agreement is appropriate to the present and future needs of the organization. Thus factors such as the time period covered by the agreement, whether it is a one-off purchase, or call-off arrangement, and the likelihood of repeat business, will all have a significant effect on the terms offered by potential suppliers. Again the views of the customers and potential suppliers will need to be taken fully into account before decisions are taken.

The following are the most common types of supply agreement:

One-off purchase

- Used where supplies are readily available and prices fluctuate frequently.
- Particularly appropriate for commodity buying.
- Used where there is little or no advantage in developing a longer term relationship with supplier.

Call-off contracts

- Negotiated with one or more suppliers for a range of products.
- Users 'call-off' requirements as needed over the period of the contract.
- Particularly suitable for large organizations with centralized buying, who can take advantage of large volume discounts.
- Facilitated by electronic systems, e.g. CHOICE, a software package developed by Belmin Systems which provides users with an electronic catalogue of products for which contracts have been set up, together with additional information on prices, quantities and suppliers (Carter, 1993).
- Suppliers are not guaranteed a specified volume of purchases, though usually estimates of uptake are provided, and higher prices may be paid to the supplier if actual uptake falls below the estimate.
- Suppliers may build in price increases to cover the risk of a low rate of call-off if there is no provision for price adjustment.

Scheduled agreements

- A specified volume or value of products is negotiated with a supplier over a period of time.
- During that period, deliveries are scheduled on a regular basis to meet the organization's requirement.

Duration of supply agreements

Other than for one-off purchases, the judgement as to whether the agreement should be short or long term depends on a number of factors.

Short-term agreements are typically for 1 year or less, possibly with the option to renew, and are appropriate:

- For non-critical products for which there are many suppliers and there may price advantages in frequent testing of the market.
- Where there are low risks of non-supply or price fluctuation; but there is no incentive for the supplier to improve quality, achieve cost reductions or engage in supplier development.

However, in using short-term agreements you may incur high costs in renegotiating the contract or selecting a new supplier.

The duration of long-term agreements may vary:

- Between products, e.g. an agreement to develop a critical new component for an aircraft or car could be for 10–15 years.
- Between sectors, e.g. in the public sector, agreements over 2 years would be regarded as long term.
- Between products and services, e.g. service contracts in the public sector vary between 4 and 7 years, due to the high costs of renegotiation and high investment required by contractors.

Long-term contracts provide the opportunity to ensure improving quality, achieve cost reductions and engage in supplier development. However, they may carry greater risks of non-supply or price fluctuation.

In order to reduce the cost of unnecessarily frequent purchases, you should seek to extend the range of materials, goods and services covered by long-term, periodic contracts wherever possible. However, the longer the term of the contract, the more important it is that you calculate the life-cycle costs of the contract, including running costs, maintenance and discounted values, accurately. The risks to price stability and the survival of the supplier are of course increased over a longer term, and therefore you should build into the supply agreement provision for review and adjustment of price and quantity supplied. You can also use life-cycle costing to decide between buying or leasing, to determine when to finalize an agreement, or decide on the duration of agreement (see Chapter 8 for a fuller discussion).

You may also wish to establish payment mechanisms and strategies prior to selection of suppliers. These may range from laying down a preference to trade only with suppliers who can link into the organization's electronic ordering, invoicing and accounting systems, to very specific policies on the number of days allowed for payment (see Chapter 9).

Summary

This chapter has examined the processes involved in planning and specifying supply requirements. These processes identify the range and volume of products and services to be bought in, as well as providing a detailed outline of their physical and performance characteristics. We have emphasized the importance of the role of customers and, increasingly, suppliers in these processes. The benefits of adopting an integrated, team approach involving contributions from various departments other than purchasing, have also been highlighted. Chapter 8 examines how you may select suppliers for the organization's requirements and, in particular, explores formal tendering procedures.

Activities

1

Your Purchasing Manager has asked you to prepare a guide outlining how purchasing requirements for the organization are planned. You should identify how purchasing plans relate to overall organizational objectives, and how the needs of internal customers, other departments or functions are incorporated.

2

Your Purchasing Manager is concerned that specifications for products and services are being prepared by internal customers without taking into account the consequences in terms of cost, lack of competition, performance, etc. You are asked to draft a memo outlining key points for internal customers to consider when specifying their requirements, and the benefits for budget holders which will ensue.

References and further reading

Baily, P. (1991) *Purchasing Systems and Records*, 3rd edn, Gower, Aldershot

Barker, L. (1993) *Competing for Quality: a Manager's Guide to Market Testing*, Longman, Harlow

Burt, D. N. (1989) 'Managing product quality through strategic purchasing', *Sloan Management Review*, **Spring**, 39–48

Carter, A. (1993) 'Bristol hospitals put their trust in Unix database', *Purchasing and Supply Management*, December, 22–23

Davies, O. (1985) 'Strategic purchasing', in Farmer, D. (ed.), *Purchasing Management Handbook*, Gower, London

Lyons, M. T. and Johnson, A. (1993) *Preparing the Winning Bid: A Handbook for Competitive Tendering*, Charles Knight, Croydon

Lysons, C. K. (1993) *Purchasing*, 3rd edn, M & E Handbooks/Pitman, London

Office of Public Service and Science (1993) *The Government's Guide to Market Testing*, HMSO, London

8 Supplier selection

Introduction

Supplier selection is central to the work of all buyers, and is probably the most important function in the purchasing process. How frequently you carry out selection processes will vary depending on how many contracts you are responsible for, and whether they are long or short term. How they are carried out will also vary between organizations which engage in partnership sourcing and select suppliers through negotiation, and those organizations which adopt a competitive tendering approach. This chapter explores the issues surrounding this important process and the procedures through which it is carried out.

The aims of this chapter are therefore to:

- Examine how potential suppliers may be identified.
- Consider the criteria for selection which may be used.
- Assess the relative merits of and factors affecting methods of supplier selection.
- Outline procedures followed in competitive tendering.
- Explore post-tender clarification and improvement of offers.

Supplier selection process

A helpful chart of the steps in the selection of suppliers is presented in Figure 8.1. This indicates the options to be considered, in particular whether it is a one-off or regular purchase, whether a contract has already been set up from which users may call off their requirements, and whether there is a need to test the market to assure the competitiveness of supply. Unless there is already an annual contract set up against which an order can be made, there is a need to identify possible sources of supply.

Identification of potential suppliers

Having specified the product or service to be supplied, and the nature of the supply agreement, potential suppliers may be identified. You may recall that sources of information on the supply market were identified in Chapter 2. Those most likely to be used in identifying suitable potential suppliers are:

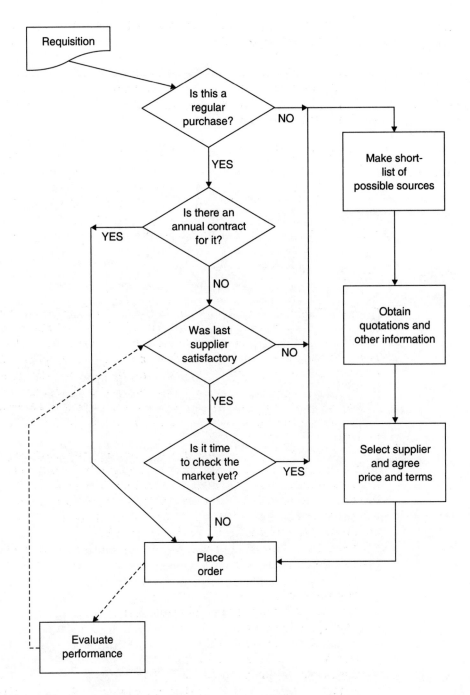

Figure 8.1 Source selection model. (From P. Baily, *Purchasing Systems and Records*, 3rd edn, Gower, Aldershot, p. 22, 1991)

- Current and past supplier records, particularly from vendor appraisal and vendor rating systems.
- Customers.
- Company directories and buyer guides.
- Trade journals for the product or industry.
- Suppliers' representatives or literature.
- Trade fairs and exhibitions.

The number of potential suppliers can vary in theory from one, perhaps a partnership supplier with which you wish to extend the scope of your agreement to further products or services, to an infinite number of possible respondents to an open tender. You need to make sure that the number and range of potential suppliers identified are appropriate for the specified supplies and sufficient to test the market.

Criteria for selection

In many organizations, especially those in the public sector, it is important that you identify potential suppliers correctly. You need therefore to establish the criteria for selection of the successful supplier. These may include a balanced assessment of factors such as price, quantity, quality standards, carriage and delivery time and location, maintenance and after-sales service, method of payment, and terms of payment. The EC Public Procurement Directives stipulate two criteria, either price, or the most economically advantageous offer (see below for a fuller discussion of criteria allowable under the Directives).

As we saw in Chapter 3, some organizations operate select lists, or lists of approved suppliers, the process of selection for which must conform to the EC Directives on Public Procurement if they apply to your organization. You therefore need to identify clearly the criteria for selection of those suppliers invited to quote, and allow opportunities for those suppliers not on an approved list to be considered on future occasions.

Criteria for inclusion on a select list of suppliers for a typical public sector organization may include:

- Employee assessment procedures.
- Number of employees in relevant work.
- Staff qualifications.
- Registration for BS 5750.
- Quality of technical references.
- Satisfactory financial position.
- Whether there are any outstanding claims or litigation against the company.
- Adequacy of insurance.
- Health and safety policy.
- Compliance with relevant employment legislation.

INVESTIGATE

- *How do you identify the suppliers which you may invite to bid or negotiate for supply? What criteria do you use for their selection?*

Methods of selection

This section examines the merits of and main factors affecting methods of selecting suppliers, through inviting bids, tenders and direct negotiation with one or more potential suppliers. These are not of course mutually exclusive, as some negotiation may also take place where bids or tenders are invited.

Bids

You may invite bids from a small, often specified, number of suppliers for low-value purchases, without the formalities and cost of tendering. If your organization has a supplier appraisal scheme, you may invite bids from only those suppliers of a product which have achieved a high rating. Potential suppliers are invited to bid against the specification, either verbally or in writing. However, you still need to obtain bids in a form allowing for comparison, and in accordance with agreed procedures and time-table.

Tenders

This is a much more formal approach, normally with time-scales, documentation and evaluation procedures laid down either by legislation or organizational rules. Detailed procedures are examined below. First, though, we will look at arguments for and against competitive bidding:

Arguments in favour of competitive bidding include:
- It enables the buyer to obtain the lowest price for his requirements, as the knowledge that he is competing with other firms compels each bidder to quote as low as possible in order to win the business.
- It provides an equitable and objective method of assessing suppliers.
- It ensures compliance with accountability to taxpayers and shareholders.
- It provides transparency and an audit trail to justify supplier selection.
- It protects against fraud and ensures ethical practice.

Arguments against competitive bidding include:
- The lowest-price bidder may be forced to cut quality to achieve the bid price.
- The winning bidder often removes the competition provided either in-house or by competitors in the marketplace, and can conse-

quently achieve a monopoly position and increase prices in the subsequent tendering process.

- The difficulties, expense and time associated with switching to new suppliers.
- Expectations of competition may be false, especially in markets with one or a few dominant suppliers.
- There are high transaction costs in terms of detailed procedures, records, and documents.
- It lengthens the time required to obtain supplies.
- Tendering regulations may hinder efficient purchasing, as accepting offers entirely on the basis of the lowest tendered price may prevent the achievement of broader 'value-for-money' performance.

Many of these arguments for and against competitive tendering are conditional upon the nature of the supplier market and how the process is carried out. You can check whether use of competitive tendering is efficient and effective against the following conditions:

- Are there many sellers, or at least the potential for market entry or substitutes in a concentrated market (see Chapter 3)?
- Is the value of the specific purchase sufficiently large to justify the high transaction costs?
- Is the specification explicit and clear to both buyer and seller, and does it identify criteria for selection?
- Will a broad range of financial, technical and managerial criteria be used in the evaluation of tenders?
- Are the sellers technically qualified, actively seeking the contract, and therefore willing to price competitively?
- Will there be sufficient time allowed for bidders to prepare bids, especially new suppliers?
- Is formal tendering to be accompanied by pre- and post-tender negotiation, conducted in accordance with ethical practice (see below)?

Negotiation

We will see later in this chapter that tendering and negotiation are not mutually exclusive, though strict rules may be laid down to govern the scope and conduct of tendering, especially in the public sector. Selection of supplier by negotiation alone is often associated with a partnership approach, where existing, long-term suppliers will be given the first opportunity to discuss the supply of a new product, usually at an early stage in its design.

The advantages of negotiation are:

- Reduced time spent looking for new suppliers and gathering competitive bids.

- Continuity of relationships with suppliers who are aware of your needs and way of doing business.
- Reduced risks for both suppliers and customer organization, and should as a result lead to reduced costs.
- Incentives for suppliers to invest in electronic and manufacturing systems compatible with those of the customer organization.

However, possible disadvantages include:

- Increased danger of collusion and fraud.
- Increased difficulty of evaluating offers on an equal basis.
- No guarantee that the outcome of the negotiation will be competitive in relation to the supply market.
- Selection may be discriminatory under EC Public Procurement Directives for public sector organizations and the utilities, unless use of the negotiated procedure is permitted.

Negotiation styles and strategies are examined in Chapter 9. The rest of this chapter considers tendering rules and procedures in greater detail.

| INVESTIGATE |

- *How does your organization select its suppliers? Is the process governed by legislation, organizational rules and procedures? How efficient and effective is it?*

Competitive tendering rules and procedures

EC Public Procurement Directives

The opening up of public procurement to competition from all member states was an integral part of the European Single Market programme. The procurement directives require transparency and non-discrimination in the tendering process, and hence tenders have to be advertised in the *Official Journal of the EC* together with the award criteria which will be used, as does notice of the award itself after it has been made.

The EC procurement directives are:

- *Supplies Directive* (Directive 93/36). This covers the purchase, lease and hire of goods by central governments, local and regional authorities in respect of contracts equal to or over 200 000 ECUs (£149 728 for regional and local governments) and 128 771 ECUs (£96 403) for central government and other bodies subject to the General

Agreement on Tariff and Trade (GATT) Government Procurement Agreement.

- *Works Directive* (Directive 93/37). This applies to contracts involving construction or civil engineering works for central government, local and regional authorities, health and other public bodies in respect of contracts equal to or over 5 million ECUs (£3.74 million).
- *The Utilities Directive* (93/38) covering procurement of supplies, services and works in the energy, water, transport and telecommunications sectors. The threshold for supplies and services in telecommunications is 600 000 ECUs (£449 184), whilst for the other sectors covered it is 400 000 ECUs (£229 456). The threshold for utilities works is the same as in the Works directive.
- *The Services Directive* (92/50). This covers priority services with a threshold of 200 000 ECUs (£149 728). Priority services include banking and insurance, consultancy, advertising, computing and accounting.

See Cox (1993) and O'Loan (1992a,b, 1994) for a fuller discussion of the provisions of the directives.

The directives provide three ways in which contracts can be awarded:

- *Open procedure*: any supplier may tender.
- *Restricted procedure*: any supplier may apply to be considered; the purchaser then selects suppliers he thinks capable of competing and invites them to tender.
- *Negotiated procedures*: direct discussions take place between the purchaser and one or more suppliers of the purchaser's choice; this procedure may only be used in strictly specified circumstances.

The directives allow purchasers to apply either of two criteria in the selection of bids:

- Price alone.
- A combination of factors which result in the tender being the most economically advantageous.

Box 8.1 shows a tender advert that complies with the EC Public Sector Supplies Directive. This is extracted from the Tenders European Daily Service (TEDS), which provides an electronic database of contracts advertised in the Official Journal of the EC. The contract is to be awarded by the open procedure, for a fixed price, and full information on qualification of suppliers is provided under Section 12. Note that the contracting authority cannot require suppliers to be registered in the United Kingdom or Ireland alone, but must make the contract open to companies registered in any of the member states. The award criterion is the most economically advantageous offer, and the various elements to be taken into account are specified in Section 13. However, no estimate of the value of the contract is given.

Box 8.1 *Tender advertisement in compliance with EC Public Procurement Directives*

14 00/000001 ECHO: -TED /COPYRIGHT ECHO

TI: UK – Ballycastle, vehicles; DT: 940916 12 00
ND: 50728-94 BASE TEDA; JO S 146; PP. 0064; PD 940802
TD: 3 – Invitation to tender;
LD: EN.
NC: 2 – Supply contract.
PR: 1 – Open procedure.
RP: 4 – EEC.
AA: 3 – Local authorities.
TY: 3 – Mixed 1 and 2 bid.
CY: GB.
AC: 2 – Most economic bid
CC: 3510 – MOTOR VEHICLES AND THEIR ENGINES (INCLUDING ROAD TRACTORS)
AU: MOYLE DISTRICT COUNCIL
DD: 940826 16 00
TX: 1 Awarding authority: Moyle District Council, Sheskburn House, 7 Mary Street, UK – Ballycastle BT54 6QH.
Tel. (026 57) 622 25. Facsimile (026 57) 625 15.
2 (a) Award procedure: Open procedure.
  (b) Contract type: Purchase.
3 (a) Delivery to: UK – Ballycastle.
  (b) Goods, CPA reference number: 2, 26-tonne gross vehicle weight refuse collection vehicles.
  (c) Division into lots: Suppliers can tender for 1 or more parts of the supplies required.
4 Delivery deadline: To be determined at the time of order.
5 (a) Documents from: As in (1) Mr. T. Stuart, Technical Services Manager.
  (b) Requests not later than: 26/8/1994 (16.00).
  (c) Fee: None.
6 (a) Deadline for receipt of tenders: 16/9/1994 (12.00).
  (b) Address: As in (1), Mr. R. G. Lewis, B.Sc.(Econ) I.P.F.A., Clerk and Chief Executive, quoting reference 'vehicle tender'.
  (c) Language(s): English.
7 (a) Opening of tenders (persons admitted): The clerk and chief executive and council officers.
  (b) Date, time and place: 16/9/1994 (14.00). As in (1).
8
9 Financing and payment: Fixed price contract.
10
11 Qualifications: Certificate of enrolment on the professional or trade register under the conditions laid down by the laws of the Member State in which he is established, for instance on the Register of Companies in the United Kingdom and Ireland, or declaration on oath or solemn declaration. List of the principal deliveries effected in the past 3 years, with the sums, dates and recipients, public or private, involved.
Indication of the technicians or technical bodies involved, whether or not belonging directly to the undertaking, especially those responsible for quality control.
Samples, description and/or photographs of the products to be supplied.
Certificates drawn up by official quality control institutes or agencies.
12 Tenders may lapse after: 2 months starting 22/7/1994.
13 Award criteria (other than price): Economically most advantageous tender in terms of price, delivery date, running costs, quality, technical merit, after-sales service and technical back-up.
14
15
16
17 Notice postmarked: 19/7/1994.
18 Notice received on: 19/7/1994.

Source: Tenders Electronic Daily, *copyright ECHO, PO Box 2373, L-1023 Luxembourg*

It is clear that the EC Directives dictate the use of competitive tendering. This is particularly evident in the emphasis on formal tendering procedures, on attracting bids from suppliers throughout the EC, and on maintaining an arms-length relationship with suppliers. Some flexibility is, however, provided in the selection criteria by the opportunity to specify the most economically advantageous offer rather than lowest price alone. Whilst there is also provision for the negotiated procedure, its use is heavily circumscribed.

In the public sector, where procurement may be used as an instrument of economic or social policy, criteria for selection may give preference to small businesses, minority groups, or suppliers from designated regions. Such preferential treatment may be contrary to the EC Directives, a belief which led in August 1994 to the UK government scrapping the Priority Suppliers Scheme which gave priority to disabled workers for certain types of goods.

To date, the EC Directives have not resulted in a significant increase in the cross-national award of contracts within the EC (see for instance Hartley and Uttley, 1994). It is too early in the operation of the directives to state definitively whether this is as a result of non-compliance, or structural factors in European markets which result in national suppliers retaining an advantage over competitors from other countries. However, the European Commission is stepping up its monitoring of compliance, and there is evidence that contracting authorities are increasingly complying with the procedures, even if the outcomes still seem to favour national suppliers!

Compulsory competitive tendering by local authorities

Successive Local Government Acts (1980, 1988, 1989, 1991) have imposed a duty on local authorities to tender their services competitively. These prescribe:

- General arrangements for conducting compulsory competitive tendering (CCT), including the organizational split between client and contractor (see Chapter 7).
- Those functions to be subject to CCT.
- The time-table for implementation.
- Accounting practices, e.g. what costs can and cannot be included by in-house teams bidding for a contract.
- The rates of return required.

Procedures are similar to those outlined in Figure 7.1.

Services subject to CCT rules include:

- Building maintenance.
- Refuse collection.
- Street cleansing.
- Grounds maintenance.
- Vehicle maintenance.
- Sport and leisure.

The 1991 Act extended the rules to cover 'professional' services such as personnel, finance, legal and computing to be implemented progressively over subsequent years.

Many critics argue that the strong emphasis on competitive tendering obstructs the achievement of efficient and effective purchasing, particularly in respect of developing close, long-term partnership relationships with key suppliers. There is evidence, however, that CCT has resulted in reduced cost of service provision, even though approximately 80% of service contracts have been won by in-house teams. Critics argue that this is at the cost of cuts in numbers of staff and their terms and conditions, although there is no convincing evidence of reduced service quality or levels. Indeed, there is evidence of technical and logistical innovation, for example the use of more advanced equipment and logistics in refuse collection, which suggests that the threat of competition *is* capable of generating improved performance.

INVESTIGATE

- *Is your organization covered by either or both of the above areas of legislation? If so, do you know the procedures which you are required to follow? Do you think they achieve efficient and effective purchasing? If not, how might they be improved, either in their operation or in their requirements?*

Tender documentation

The amount of detail provided will vary considerably with the nature of the product or service. A fairly straightforward example relating to standard office furniture is provided below (see Box 8.2). However, an extreme case is the tender documentation associated with the new rail link from London to connect with the Channel Tunnel, which was reported to weigh half a ton! Whilst the specification will vary, the accompanying documentation will most likely include the following:

- Conditions of tender:
  - Instructions for tendering
  - Form of agreement
  - Financial guarantees required, e.g. bonds, parent company indemnity, bank reference
  - Statement of partners'/directors' names and addresses
  - Outline of management structures, details of staff qualifications
  - Trading history and circumstances
  - Insurance, e.g. third party, employer's liability
  - Completed pricing schedule or bill of quantities (if applicable)
  - Compliance with legislation, e.g. equal opportunities, health and safety at work.

- Conditions of contract (see Chapter 9).
- Service specification (see Chapter 7).
- Service standards (see Chapter 7).
- Pricing mechanism.
  - Indices of materials costs
  - Indices of labour costs
  - Retail Price Index
  - A combination of indices weighted in accordance with their contribution to overall costs.
- Evaluation criteria
  - Preliminary evaluation, to weed out any tenders which do not comply with the formal requirements of the tender process
  - Assessment against selection criteria, e.g. administrative, technical or financial.

Tenders received must be recorded and opened according to prescribed organizational procedures and legal requirements.

Whilst the use of tendering is normally associated with the public sector, it is also practised extensively in the private sector, as the following examples demonstrate. The first shows that the formalities of tendering, such as anonymity of bidders, strict deadlines for return, and a concern for fairness, are observed just as closely in the private as in the public sector.

Tendering procedure at IBM

We draw up the specification with users, invite bids, specify criteria, including performance and quality measurements, and agree with users who the appropriate bidders are. Then we put the quotation pack together, and it is sent to vendors with coded numbers, to be returned by the due date. Bids are then opened, and the buyers make their recommendations. We then call together a panel of users, and invite oral bids from a shortlist of suppliers. Then we apply the evaluation criteria (including the cost of changes), add in our impression of the oral presentations and agree the appropriate supplier. Throughout the process we seek to maintain a clear view that is fair to the suppliers – to demonstrate fairness.

Source: Interview, Purchasing Manager, IBM UK Ltd

The oral presentations allow the suppliers an opportunity to explain their bids, and enable the purchasing staff and users to clarify aspects of the bid or the suppliers' business. The formalities are also in evidence in the next example.

Buying consultancy services at British Airways

I would discuss with the Purchasing Manager what consultants are needed. I have an approved list of quantity surveyors, etc. If the size of the job requires going out to tender, I put out a letter inviting fee proposals, agree time for them to put in bids, have tender opening procedure, record everything on to a standard tender report, which has all the information about the project. We assess price, quality, value, then invite the top two to discuss their fee proposals in detail: scope of books, resource structure, etc. We decide together on the right company – the purchaser makes the commitment, but the Senior Buyer can only contract up to £25 000. Above this, it goes to the Contracts Committee, with people from maintenance, construction, purchasing, etc. We need to justify the decision. If the recommendation is approved, I contact the consultant. The letter of appointment is sent out; the form of contract is already included in a letter of invitation.

Source: Interview, Senior Buyer, Construction, British Airways

---

The next example shows a method of preventing the financial data, especially price, distorting the overall assessment of tenders, as well as the use of criteria weighted to reflect the assessors' perceptions of their importance.

Buying property-related services at IBM

We bring people together, including engineering experts, people who will work as a team, analyse the tender data, present to the team; various costs, other areas require further analysis. We tried it a new way – gave out copies of quotes minus numerical data, out of 15 points rated high/medium/low, with a rating system of 1 to 5 for each supplier, and ranked them according to systems, approach, management expertise, then plotted each person's results. We gave each quote a total score, then showed the financial data and compared them to the ratings. Usually the highest rating has the highest cost. Then we shortlist suppliers, look at the financial data, e.g. labour ratios, pay rate to operatives, special conditions, e.g. BUPA membership. For each supplier we have notes for the meeting which are prepared and distributed. When the suppliers come in we reduce the numbers from IBM, only the senior engineer, agree notes for the meetings, users recognize that it is purchasing's responsibility, buyer leads supplier analysis

> meeting, use critique again to re-evaluate the proposal, get second
> rating which usually decides which supplier is selected.
>
> *Source: Interview, Buyer, IBM UK Ltd*

Thus the highest rated, i.e. best overall bid, is often the highest priced, which indicates that assessing bids on price alone does not result in the selection of the best supplier.

One significant common feature of the above examples is that, whilst the buyer leads the tendering and evaluation process, it is a team effort, involving representatives from users (internal customers) and other relevant departments.

Employment consequences of service contracts

Under the Transfer of Undertakings (Protection of Employment) laws (TUPE) the employment rights of staff providing a service which is contracted out or sold by their employer are guaranteed. UK law has been successfully challenged in recent cases before Industrial Tribunals with reference to the EC Acquired Rights Directive, with the result that many service contracts let by public sector authorities are now subject to TUPE. The main implication for buyers responsible for outsourcing service contracts previously carried out in-house is in terms of price. Potential contractors, including an in-house team, will need to build in the costs of maintaining the current employment conditions of staff. Should any bidder not do so, they should be discounted, or at least required to adjust their bids accordingly. You should not regard cut-price bids which ignore TUPE as an opportunity to make substantial savings, because if TUPE does apply, it may be enforced retrospectively, and the contract price will not cover the contractor against the additional costs. Added to this, a workforce which is transferred with lower employment conditions, or which loses pension rights, may not be a very contented one, which may have an effect on service quality. Therefore it is important that you establish what employment conditions are included in bids, so that their evaluation is on an equal basis.

Tender evaluation

Through the evaluation process, you need to identify not just the contractor with the lowest tender price, but also the contractor which can demonstrate technical competence, strong managerial ability, a good track record and, most importantly, overall value for money against the selection criteria.

Problems associated with tender evaluation include:

- Insufficient criteria to enable a fair comparison to be made.
- Lack of experienced staff to evaluate the tenders properly.

- Spotting the strategic tenderers.
- Encouraging competitive bids.
- Documenting all the decisions.
- Having all the relevant information available.

You may evaluate offers only against the criteria stated in the tender advert. These may relate to the conditions of supply, or to more general organizational objectives. Conditions of supply may include any combination of price, quantity, quality standards, carriage and delivery time and location, maintenance and after-sales service, method of payment and terms of payment. In practice, a more limited range of criteria will be considered, usually price at various quantities and delivered to a specified location at agreed times against quality standards. Organizational objectives may include policy on standardization, stock and turnover and rationalization of the supplier base.

It is important that you document decisions and reasons fully, and communicate the outcome promptly to users, suppliers and other interested parties. Where appropriate, the performance rating of existing suppliers may be used in the selection of suppliers.

Box 8.2 provides a practical example of tender evaluation in relation to office furniture, which illustrates some of the principles outlined above.

Other criteria which you may need to take into account in evaluating bids for more complex products include:

- Whether the product exceeds the specification.
- Results of tests on the product or a sample thereof.
- Duration of guarantees or warranties.
- Whether there is a direct ordering or call-off facility.
- Whether the price includes supply, offloading, assembly and installation.
- Length of period for which price is fixed.
- Price revision formulae.
- BS 5750 or other quality standards.
- Whether there is a direct relationship or one via a distributor.
- Long-term availability of product and spares.

Life-cycle costing

You may need to use life-cycle costing and risk assessment techniques in the analysis of offers in respect of goods or services over a number of years. Life-cycle costing takes into account the running costs, maintenance and depreciation of any capital goods purchased, discounted at agreed rates for the anticipated number of years' use. However, reliable data on such costs is difficult to obtain, and information provided by suppliers may be optimistic. Risk assessment may also be used to calculate the sensitivity of the potential source to adverse developments, such as currency or commodity price fluctuations, political upheaval and natural disasters. Whilst such techniques are

Box 8.2 *Tender evaluation exercise*

As the buying section of Melchester Council you have been requisitioned to purchase a quantity of eight desks of two different types:

- Three 1600 mm width
- Five 1400 mm width

for which a specification has been established by the user.

The user requires the desks to be delivered within three weeks to coincide with a relocation of staff to new council offices.

You are required to evaluate the quotations received and present recommendations for the award of the contract based on the following information:

	Supplier 1	Supplier 2	Supplier 3
1600 mm desks	£75.70 each	£87.80 each	£93.00 each
1400 mm desks	£60.60 each	£61.90 each	£72.00 each
Delivery			
1600 mm desks	2 weeks	1 week	1 week
1400 mm desks	4 weeks	1 week	1 week

In addition, Supplier 2 requires payment in 30 days and has a delivery charge of £5 per item. Supplier 3 offers 10% discount for payment within 14 days of delivery and delivery charges are included in the unit prices. Supplier 1 requires payment within 60 days and requires a delivery charge of £50 per delivery.

Criteria for selection

You may assume that all three suppliers have been fully assessed and found acceptable, and that the items offered comply with the specification. The quality and appearance of the desks are equal. Price, delivery and payment are therefore the criteria which will distinguish the suppliers.

Evaluation matrix

It is usually helpful to present the results of the evaluation in a matrix so that all the information relevant to the evaluation can be compared more easily.

	Supplier 1	Supplier 2	Supplier 3
1600 mm desks (3)	£227.10	£263.40	£279.00
1400 mm desks (5)	£303.00	£309.50	£360.00
Total	£530.10	£572.90	£639.00
Delivery	2 weeks (1600 mm) 4 weeks (1400 mm)	1 week	1 week
Charges	£100 (2 × £50)	£40 (8 × £5)	Included
Payment	60 days	30 days	10% discount within 14 days
Total cost	£630.10	£612.90	£575.10

Supplier 1 is rejected because it cannot meet the specified delivery requirement of within 3 weeks.

Suppliers 2 and 3 meet the delivery requirements, but the early payment discount offered by Supplier 3 results in a lower price.

Supplier 3 should therefore be selected, unless the accounts department is unable to meet a 14-day payment, in which case Supplier 2 would be preferred.

speculative and cannot replace the judgement of the purchaser, they should be seen as an aid to decision. In a large organization complex analysis of major purchases would clearly require the support of a research unit, but understanding of the techniques and their application should be within the capability of most purchasers.

Life-cycle costing usually involves the following steps:

- Identification of all known costs of the agreement, e.g. purchase price, running costs, service/maintenance costs, administrative costs, costs of delivery, etc.
- Identification and weighting of the risk factors in order of priority, e.g, security of supply, quality variations, price variations, costs of borrowing, competing products.
- Calculating the future costs of agreement, using discount factors to determine which option is the most economical and effective.
- Application of the weighted risk factors to known costs in order to assess the sensitivity of the outcome.
- Selection of the option which provides the best overall investment, and is not unduly susceptible to risk.
- Should the risk factors change the outcome of the calculation, a judgement is required as to whether to ignore them or to accord them a lower significance.

Therefore, you should not regard the outcome of a life-cycle cost analysis as providing a straightforward guide to action based on the quantitative calculations. It is an aid to decision, but ultimately you have to make a judgement as to the importance of the risk factors over a number of years ahead, and decide whether the benefits of a lower initial price outweigh the costs of increased maintenance, shorter product life, extra running costs, etc. These issues are illustrated in Box 8.3.

Clarification and improvement of offers

There may be scope for clarification and improvement of the offers made. In all cases you need to query variances from specification, if necessary seeking advice from customers and technical staff. You may also need to resolve any queries relating to the conditions of supply, such as delivery and payment terms. Post-tender negotiation (PTN) is a means of ensuring that neither you nor your potential suppliers have any illusions or misunderstandings as to the exact obligations under the terms of any order or contract. It is not a licence to indulge in unprincipled and unethical standards of buying. It is a technique which buyers can use to improve value for money.

You may wish to use PTN when:

- The final bid evaluation fails to highlight one particular supplier.
- Doubt exists regarding quality, performance, conditions, etc.

Box 8.3 *Life-cycle cost analysis of photocopiers*

You are considering bids to supply a photocopier, the working life of which is estimated at 5 years, with no residual value at the end of that period. The purchase price of Copier A is £50 000, and that of Copier B £40 000. However, you are aware that Copier A is of better quality and has a better reliability record than Copier B. The cost of maintenance contracts, including spares, for the copiers reflects this, at 10% and 15% of purchase price per year, respectively. These costs need to be discounted over the 5 years at, say, 10% per year.

	Copier A	Copier B
Year 1	£5000	£6000
Year 2	£4500	£5400
Year 3	£4050	£4860
Year 4	£3645	£4374
Year 5	£3281	£3937
Total	£20 471	£24 571

Copier B also requires more frequent replacement of consumable products such as toner. The estimated costs are £1000 and £1500 per year for Copiers A and B, respectively. These costs are also discounted over the 5-year period.

	Copier A	Copier B
Year 1	£1000	£1500
Year 2	£900	£1350
Year 3	£810	£1215
Year 4	£729	£1094
Year 5	£656	£985
Total	£4095	£6144

In addition to the above quantifiable costs, there is also the very important issue of the proportion of time for which each copier is available for use. This may be calculated from your own or other organization's previous experience of the machines, from the manufacturers' estimates, or from surveys published in trade journals. Estimates of downtime for Copiers A and B are 5% and 15% respectively. This may be considered alongside the quantified costs, and a judgement made about whether the additional downtime of Copier B is sufficient to outweigh the still positive cost comparison (of approximately £4500) with Copier A. However, as the function of the copier is to produce copies, the additional downtime means that it is wasting that proportion of the total costs expended whilst it is not available. Thus you might aid your judgement by calculating the cost of the downtime in terms of total costs of both copiers, as in 'Cost of downtime' below.

	Copier A	Copier B
Purchase price (incl. delivery)	£50 000	£40 000
Maintenance (over 5 years)	£20 471	£24 571
Consumables	£4095	£6144
Total	£74 461	£70 715
Cost of downtime	£3723	£10 577
Overall cost	£78 184	£81 292

Thus the outcome of the analysis is that Copier A is the better deal, as long as you think the cost estimates are reliable. In this case the outcome is fairly close, and you may be prepared to accept the lesser quality of Copier B in return for a £10 000 saving in purchase price; the interest on which would remove the difference on discounted cost with Copier A. But it is important that you are able to carry out such calculations, even if it is only very roughly, as an aid to deciding between bids for products or services which have cost consequences for several years into the future.

- Prices offered are greater than those identified as competitive by your own analysis or through a price monitoring service.

However, you need to make sure that PTN does not become a 'Dutch auction'. It must be carefully planned and managed so that confidence and trust in the purchaser are maintained. You need to ensure, therefore, that the following conditions are observed:

- Senior management's prior approval is obtained.
- Negotiations are conducted by trained and experienced purchasing staff.
- Negotiations are fully documented, so that there is a clear audit trail.
- A precise record of all exchanges, both written and verbal, is maintained.
- Management approval for the award of the contract is obtained.

INVESTIGATE

- *Under what circumstances does your organization allow you to engage in post-tender negotiation? Is it used as a means of squeezing suppliers' margins? If so, what are the consequences in terms of supplier loyalty and repeat business? On the other hand, are you too restricted in the scope of the negotiations that you may engage in?*

Summary

This chapter has examined the process of supplier selection, in particular the relative merits of competitive bidding and negotiation in achieving competitive, efficient and effective supply. Negotiation will be examined more closely in Chapter 9, but we have seen that the procedures followed in competitive tendering, whilst time consuming, are directed at ensuring equity and fairness in the placing of contracts. This is particularly the case in respect of public sector contracts, where accountability for the use of taxpayers' money dictates strict adherence to government rules and legislation. However, tendering is also used in the private sector to maintain the competitiveness of supply, and may be combined with post-tender negotiation or clarification of offers, in order to ensure that the supplier offering the best overall product or service is selected.

Activities

1 As the Purchasing Officer of a public sector organization, you are required to source three grades of fuel oil, which will be delivered to various locations within the jurisdiction of the organization. The annual spend on this item is currently £620 000 and it has been decided that tenders will be obtained for a 2-year contract. Prepare an Invitation to Tender for this item in compliance with EC legislation.

2 Write a brief guide for buyers in your organization on how the conflicting aims of 'improving the offer' and maintaining ethical standards may be reconciled.

References and further reading

Barker, L. (1993) *Competing for Quality: a Manager's Guide to Market Testing*, Longman, Harlow

Cox, A. (1993) *The Single Market Rules and the Enforcement Regime After 1992*, Earlsgate Press, Hull

Ellram, L. M. (1993) 'Total cost of ownership: elements and implementation', *International Journal of Purchasing and Materials Management*, **Autumn**, 3–10

Hartley, K. and Uttley, M. R. H. (1994) 'The Single European Market and Public Procurement Policy: the case of the United Kingdom', *Public Procurement Law Review*, 3, 114–125

Lyons, M. T. and Johnson, A. (1992) *Preparing the Winning Bid: A Handbook for Competitive Tendering*, Charles Knight, Croydon

O'Loan, N. (1992a) 'An analysis of the Works and Supplies Directives of the European Communities', *Public Procurement Law Review*, 1, 40–55

O'Loan, N. (1992b) 'An analysis of the Utilities Directives of the European Communities', *Public Procurement Law Review*, 3, 175–188

O'Loan, N. (1994) 'United Kingdom implementation of the Services Directive 92/50', *Public Procurement Law Review*, 3 (2), CS60–68

Sparke, A. (1993) *The Compulsory Competitive Tendering Guide*, Butterworth, London

9 Contracting for supply

Introduction

In the previous chapter, various methods of supplier selection were examined, in particular competitive tendering. Even in this most adversarial process, it was recognized that negotiation played a role, especially post-tender negotiation. However, in establishing or extending a partnership relationship, negotiation is at the heart of the relationship. This chapter begins by exploring the process and content of negotiation, and then examines the nature of contracts which may result. As noted in Chapter 5, partnership relationships are not necessarily formalized in legal contracts. However, in the majority of cases, you will still be dealing with suppliers on the basis of a formal contract, and will need to know what it should contain, how it should be monitored and managed, and what to do if disputes occur. Even without a formal contract, these are issues which parties to a business relationship may need to deal with through more informal mechanisms.

Therefore, the aims of this chapter are to:

- Examine negotiation styles, objectives and plans.
- Identify the content and form of contracts which may be used for an agreement to supply.
- Explore the roles of contract monitoring and management.
- Examine how to deal with contractual disputes and claims.

Negotiation of supply agreement

In many cases you may not need to use bid or tender procedures, either because of partnership arrangements or because of organizational policy on dealing with specific suppliers for specified products. You may also be able to renew existing supply agreements without the requirement for further advertising for offers. In such cases you still need to apply similar criteria relating to conditions of supply and organizational objectives as if you were involved in a competitive bidding situation. You may also test the market by opening negotiations with several potential suppliers in order to ensure the competitiveness of existing suppliers. Before opening negotiations, you need to identify a strategy for conducting the negotiations, what techniques to use, and have a clear idea of opening positions, desired outcomes and acceptable compromises.

Negotiation strategy

Various commentators have identified the use of different negotiating styles with the adversarial and partnership approaches to selection of suppliers. The adversarial approach tends to involve a win/lose or zero-sum negotiating style. Here, if one side wins, the other loses out. Power is exercised by a dominant party, perhaps a monopoly supplier, to force the terms of agreement on the dependent party (you may recall the example of the photocopier market examined in Chapter 2). If the buyer is dominant, a tendering or bidding process may result in a 'Dutch auction' to squeeze every possible concession from suppliers desperate for the business. Price is usually the dominant criterion. The award of the contract under such conditions may result in dissatisfaction on both sides, as the buyer in a monopoly market seeks to extract every possible degree of value from the high-price contract he feels he was forced to accept, or the successful supplier to a dominant buyer cuts corners to ensure that the costs of the contract do not bankrupt him. In both cases, the risk of buyer or seller opportunistically breaking the contract in order to seek a better deal elsewhere is high, and there will undoubtedly be frequent and costly disputes over the performance of the contracts. Whilst one side believes it has won, and the idea of zero-sum means that the winner gains to the extent that the loser loses, in practice the outcome is often lose–lose, or zero minus x, where x is the cost of managing or carrying out a contract imposed by a dominant party. Whilst this relates to extreme examples, even where the benefits and costs of the outcome of such a negotiation are more evenly shared, the costs of the negotiation game, and the resulting feeling of both parties that they have lost out to some extent, may result in mutual dissatisfaction. More significantly, the negotiation will ignore wider aspects of the total relationship, beyond the immediate contract, where substantial mutual benefits may be gained.

Thus the partnership approach emphasizes negotiation on the basis of win–win, or non-zero sum, where both parties gain. Preconditions for such negotiations include the recognition of mutual interests, trust in each others' intentions, openness in exchanges, especially with regard to cost information, and readiness to discuss and arbitrate any problems which arise, rather than seek recourse to lawyers and the courts.

The styles of negotiation appropriate to each of these scenarios are illustrated very effectively by Fisher et al. (1991), who distinguish between 'positional bargaining' which relates to an adversarial approach, and 'principled negotiation' which relates to a partnership approach. Box 9.1 contrasts the features of a hard form of positional bargaining with those of principled negotiation.

The main aspects of principled negotiation are given in italics in Box 9.1. Because people tend to become emotionally involved in an adversarial negotiation, you should separate the problem from the people involved, who should see themselves as working side by side to resolve it. Secondly, rather than focus on bargaining positions which cannot be satisfied, and mask

Box 9.1 *Hard positional bargaining and principled negotiation*

Positional bargaining	Principled negotiation
Participants are adversaries	Participants are problem solvers
The goal is victory	The goal is a wise outcome reached efficiently and amicably
Demand concessions as a condition of the relationship	*Separate the people from the problem*
Be hard on the problem and the people	Be soft on the people, hard on the problem
Distrust others	Proceed independent of trust
Dig into your position	*Focus on interests not positions*
Make threats	Explore interests
Mislead as to your bottom line	Avoid having a bottom line
Demand one-sided gains as the price of agreement	*Invent options for mutual gain*
Search for the single answer: the one you will accept	Develop multiple options to choose from: decide later
Insist on your position	*Insist on objective criteria*
Try to win a contest of will	Try to reach a result based on standards independent of will
Apply pressure	Reason and be open to reasons; yield to principle, not pressure

Source: Adapted from R. Fisher, W. Ury and B. Patton, Getting to Yes, *Business Books/Random Century, London, p. 13, 1991, 2nd edn.* Copyright © 1981, 1991, by Roger Fisher and William Ury. Reprinted by permission of Houghton Mifflin Co. All rights reserved.

underlying interests, you should address the interests themselves. Thirdly, rather than trying to identify the one best solution in a pressurized, antagonistic negotiation situation, both parties should seek a range of creative solutions through brainstorming, based on shared interests and the reconciliation of different interests. Fourthly, a stubborn stance by one party may be countered by seeking to establish a fair, objective standard such as 'market value, expert opinion, custom or law' on which a fair solution to which both parties can defer may be based.

For the sceptical buyer, Fisher et al. provide advice on how to deal in a principled way with negotiators who do not see the wisdom of adopting a principled approach. For example, in a situation where the other side is more powerful, they advise that you establish your 'best alternative to a negotiated agreement' (BATNA). Should the other party fail to make an offer which meets this, you should walk away from the negotiation, which in itself may result in an acceptable offer. In a situation where the other side will not engage in principled negotiation, 'negotiation jujitsu' is proposed, by which you sidestep the other party's position: rather than attack it, look behind it to their interests; rather than defend a position yourself, invite criticism and advice; and if you are attacked, recast it as an attack on the problem. Finally, they provide guidance on how to deal with the other party's dirty tricks. For example, if deliberate deception is suspected, it should be countered by seeking verification. If the other side claims full authority, only to claim further approval is necessary after apparently reaching a settlement, you should do the same, or set a deadline for agreement on the basis of the settlement. Principled negotiation is not weakness: 'You can be just as firm as they can, even firmer. It is easier to defend principle than an illegitimate tactic' (Fisher et al., 1991, p. 149)'.

How well does Fisher et al.'s approach fit with the example given below?

Negotiation

Negotiation skills are important. You need to be able to identify your own relative strengths and weaknesses and the vendors' perceived strengths and weaknesses. You have to be prepared to stick to your guns, be flexible – find ways of getting something out of a vendor, be able to give up a small thing to gain something bigger. I am often in negotiation with managing directors, for example on the car rental contract I am dealing with the European car rental director: you have to know how to feel comfortable, know when not to agree -- you don't agree too early!

Source: Interview, Purchasing Manager, IBM

The tone of this example is perhaps more adversarial than principled, although there is recognition of the need for both sides to gain something from the negotiation. In practice, various strategies may be involved, ranging across the full spectrum from adversarial to principled, even at different times in the same negotiation. Other important points raised are the need to assess strengths and weaknesses as a basis for selecting which areas of the deal you should concentrate on, and being able to deal on an equal level with more senior managers in supplier companies. This is not necessarily a matter of status, but of competence: if you have the authority to negotiate the deal, and can convince your counterpart by your approach to the negotiation that you know what you're doing, then any difference in status is irrelevant.

INVESTIGATE

- *What negotiating strategies do you employ? Do they relate more closely to adversarial or principled negotiation? Are you able to adjust your strategy to different circumstances and suppliers?*

Establishing contract for supply

Once you have selected a supplier and negotiated the terms of the deal, a contract may be drawn up. In many cases you may use the standard terms and conditions often printed on the purchasing organization's order. In all cases, however, you need to ensure that criteria establishing failure to supply and remedies are clearly stated, and that the contract offers adequate protection and acceptable risk regarding breach.

Conditions of contract

In most cases you will not as a buyer be expected to invent contract conditions, and will rely on standard terms and conditions used by the organization. These may have been drafted by your own legal experts, or developed from those of other organizations, or taken off-the-shelf from bodies such as the Chartered Institute of Purchasing and Supply (CIPS). For example, central government departments are provided with model forms of contract, a Guidance Note (No. 20) produced by the Central Unit on Procurement, and a booklet *Standard Conditions of Government Contracts for Stores Purchases* is available. Individual departments may also have standard terms and conditions which may adapt and develop this general guidance. Different contractual conditions applying to goods, works and services are also available. There may also be special contract terms applicable for specific types of purchases, such as computers, for which the Government's Central Computer and Technology Agency have produced standard form contracts, and for the purchase of consultancy services. Thus the important competence is in selecting the form of contract appropriate to the nature of the purchase, rather than in engaging in the potentially dangerous process of drafting contracts yourself. For those who do not have access to such a range of ready-made contracts, the CIPS have available model forms of contract which are available from the bookshop, together with standard texts which are noted in the references and further reading to this chapter. Common conditions of a contract for supplies are set out in Box 9.2.

Forms of contract

You may be aware of various forms of contract which may be used, each with a different balance of costs and risks between buyer and supplier (see Turpin, 1989, Chap. 6 for a good discussion of their use in government contracts). The main forms are described below.

Fixed price

The buyer agrees to pay a fixed price for the goods or services supplied. This form is typically used for a one-off purchase. Should the contract extend over a period of time with many deliveries, there are likely to be price variation

---

Box 9.2   *Common conditions of a contract for supplies*

- *Definitions:* client or buyer; contractor or seller; purchase order; the contract.
- *Specifications:* supplies to conform; buyer's right to alter.
- *Inspection of supplies:* buyer's right to.
- *Prices:* whether delivery included; to what location; discounts, e.g. prompt payment; VAT; variations.
- *Delivery:* responsibilities of supplier, e.g. secure packaging; locations; timing; rejects.
- *Terms of payment:* invoicing; when payment due.
- *Default:* buyer's right to determine; obtaining alternative supplies; liquidated damages, i.e. financial liability of supplier for default.
- *Insolvency or bankruptcy of supplier:* buyer's protection against.
- *Special conditions:* relating to supplier's observance of fair employment practices, minimum wage provisions, etc. (for government contracts).
- *Ethical provisions:* e.g. gifts, payment of commission.
- *Notices:* how forms, etc., are to be transmitted, e.g. mail, fax, electronically.
- *Law:* which country's law governs the contract, e.g. English, Scottish, Northern Irish.

Service or works contracts may in addition require the following conditions:

- *Contractor's organization:* qualifications of staff; facilities.
- *Assignment and subletting:* conditions under which allowed; payment of subcontractors.
- *Equipment:* conditions under which client's equipment may be used; ownership; contractor's responsibility for own equipment.
- *Indemnity and insurances:* contractor's responsibility to indemnify client for loss, damage, injury, and against infringement of patents, copyright, etc.; value of insurances required.
- *Monitoring and liaison:* contractor's responsibility for monitoring the contract; maintenance and submission of performance records; attendance at meetings, etc.
- *Clearance of sites on completion.*

---

clauses covering increases or decreases in inflation, exchange rates, labour costs, materials costs, etc.

Alternatively, the buyer may decide to forego the benefit of price reductions, but in return the fixed price will be lower. If the supplier decides to forego any increase in price, then the fixed price is likely to be higher to cover these risks.

Cost plus

This form of contract is used when the supplier's costs cannot be accurately estimated, particularly for long-term product development or capital projects. The supplier's actual costs will be reimbursed, together with either a fixed fee or percentage profit element. However, the cost element is likely to escalate uncontrollably as the supplier has no incentive to control costs, unless your organization has full knowledge of the supplier's costs, and the expertise to determine their necessity and accuracy. Ministry of Defence contracts were typically of this type, and led to claims that suppliers were exaggerating their costs; in some cases suppliers have been required to make repayments following investigations by the National Audit Office.

Incentive

More recently, various forms of incentives have been developed in an attempt to control costs by sharing the risks between buyer and supplier. A maximum price incentive provides the buyer with protection against cost overruns, but places most of the risk on suppliers to reduce costs, and may result in lower quality or even default. The maximum cost may also be very difficult to estimate, and will be subject to similar calculations to those used in the decision to forego price increases in fixed price contracts. Alternatively, target costs may be agreed: any savings under the target will be shared equally between the buyer and supplier, whilst either a proportion of or all excess costs may have to be borne by the supplier, with the safety net of a guaranteed minimum profit. Time-based incentives or penalties may also be provided in the case of works projects, with specified increases in payments by the buyer for early completion, and financial penalties for late completion. A celebrated example of the former was the rebuilding of the Santa Monica freeway in Los Angeles after the earthquake in 1994, which was completed several months early, and earned the contractor US$1 million for each day prior to the specified completion date. An infamous example of the latter was the late completion of the Channel Tunnel works by TransManche, which led to massive claims for compensation by Eurotunnel. Performance-based incentives may also be used, which will be higher or lower in relation to predetermined levels of performance of a product or quality of service.

A more complex form of incentive contract may determine weights for each aspect of the contract, so that the total incentive fee to be paid may be made up as follows:

Cost incentive	50%
Performance incentive	30%
Time-based incentive	20%

However, in order that incentives have the intended effect of encouraging suppliers or contractors to perform better, they should not be so complex that they cannot be expressed clearly in easily communicated targets which then motivate the behaviour of all staff concerned.

Placing the order

Whilst this may appear a rather mundane aspect of the purchasing process, it is of vital importance, as there is no valid contract until the order is properly placed. You need to make sure, therefore, that the contract or order is completed accurately. The following aspects are particularly important:

- Purchase order number.
- Issue date.
- Customer requisition number.
- Supplier name and address.
- Customer delivery location and address.
- Customer name, invoicing address and account code.
- Quantity, full description, price of goods.
- Codes, such as for products, suppliers or users, where required.
- Name and telephone numbers of customer and purchasing contacts.

You also need to ensure that proper authorization is obtained through the appropriate signatures.

The possibility of errors in such details is high, no matter how carefully orders are completed. This is particularly the case if the order marks the end of a paper chase involving an initial memo from the customer, a requisition, and a tendering or written bidding process, during which there is a strong chance of errors becoming embedded in the paperwork. Therefore it is preferable to operate an electronic system, which can automatically generate the details of customers, suppliers, account numbers, codes, etc. Thus the data only need be entered and checked once, at the requisition stage, and can be transferred automatically to electronic forms for tendering, ordering, delivery and invoicing at later stages in the purchasing process.

The order may then be transmitted to the supplier promptly in accordance with agreed targets, budgets and time-scales. You may have the option of various methods of transmission, such as mailing, fax, or electronic data interchange. As the legal status of faxed or electronic orders has been unclear, it may be necessary to post the original documentation, but to transmit the order electronically to give the supplier the go-ahead where the need for the supply is urgent. You may also need to transmit copies of the contract to the customer, stores, accounts, etc., although with an integrated electronic system this could be done electronically.

In order for a contract to be established, the order needs to be accepted by the supplier. Normally this will be indicated by the supplier signing and returning a copy of the order form. However, if this is not forthcoming, or if the supplier responds by querying your terms and conditions, the contract is not established, and the supplier's intentions need to be clarified as soon as possible. If the supplier's acceptance is subject to different terms and conditions to your own, it is not advisable to allow the contract to go ahead with the intention of challenging them at a later stage, as the last form submitted will be regarded as the legal basis for the contract.

Contract monitoring and management

In this section suppliers' conformance to the conditions of individual contracts is examined, rather than the wider approach to supplier improvement taken in Chapter 6. In particular, you will need to know about progressing or expediting deliveries, and how to deal with variations in supply and contractual claims.

Progressing deliveries

Whilst you will not be able to monitor every delivery, the extent to which suppliers are able to meet the delivery requirements laid down in the contract is an important element of supplier performance which will need to be recorded in the vendor rating system. The need for progress chasing will vary between purchases and suppliers, depending on the following factors:

- *Urgency of the need*: will a stock-out of a product which is critical to production or service performance result from late delivery?
- *Familiarity with the supplier*: you may need to pay closer attention to a new supplier than to a supplier with whom you have regular dealings.
- *Delivery performance*: you will need to monitor a supplier with a poor delivery record more closely.
- *Suppliers manufacturing products to your requirements*, rather than of standard or finished goods which may be more widely available, will require closer monitoring.
- *Where you are operating just-in-time delivery to your production line*, sophisticated electronic monitoring systems may be in place to monitor the supplier's own production process to ensure that it is keeping to the production schedule.
- *The progress of supplies being delivered from overseas* may need to be monitored whilst in transit.

Whilst progress may be monitored by personal contacts by telephone, fax or visits, you may also include as part of the terms of the contract the requirement for the supplier to submit regular progress reports. This is of particular significance in relation to service contracts, where you impose a responsibility on the contractor to manage and monitor service delivery. This will vary depending on the type of management arrangement, whether managing agent, managing contractor, or total facilities management (see Chapter 4). The service specification (Chapter 7) should provide a schedule for the frequency and extent of service performance, which you may use as the basis for checking that the contractor is complying with the terms of the contract.

Variations in supply

You are unlikely to have direct responsibility for checking that goods and services delivered accord to the specification. However, you do need to ensure that systems are in place for identifying and dealing with variations, and that you know how to operate them effectively. Variations will normally be identified at point of delivery by stores or the customer if delivered direct. You will need to investigate the cause of variations to determine whether the supplier is at fault before any action is initiated. Variations may relate to the product supplied, in which case the supplier is more likely to be at fault. This may result from the technical quality of the product itself, the quantity supplied, poor packaging, loss or damage in transit or in-store whilst awaiting delivery.

Alternatively, the variation may have arisen from clerical error or a mismatch between the supplier's administrative and delivery procedures and the customer's own goods-inward procedures. Thus the product type, quantity or delivery timing and location may be wrong because the wrong details have been placed on the order form or the supplier's delivery note. Such errors are just as expensive to rectify as those relating to deficiencies in the product itself, but are more easily avoidable through greater attention to detail, use of electronic systems and close relationships with your suppliers. Minor discrepancies due to clerical error, such as small over- or underdeliveries which do not have major consequences for storage or production, may be overlooked, especially from suppliers making frequent deliveries, so long as over the period of time covered by the contract they balance out.

The following example illustrates the nature and effects of variations in supply. What additional costs are thereby incurred?

Monitoring the performance of packaging suppliers

When goods are delivered, samples are taken and tested for odour and taint. If they are rejected, I arrange to have them collected and replaced. For example, some Quality Street cartons were wet, but the printer had overmade so he was able to cover. Otherwise we may not have made the production run, and we would have had to find something else for the factory to do. To cover wastage, an extra 3–4% is added to order quantities. We monitor supplier performance: quality, quantity (including overdeliveries), time, and suppliers get a record of their performance every 2 months. Those performing poorly may be dropped.

Source: Interview, Assistant Buyer, Nestlé Rowntree

Some of the costs of variations indicated are:

- Ordering greater quantities than required.
- Overproduction by the supplier.
- Storage by customer until return of goods.
- Transit to or collection by the supplier.
- Negotiation with supplier, delivery company, customer, etc., to identify cause of variation.

- Obtaining alternative supplies.
- Administrative procedures to record variations and adjust records.
- In the worst case, loss of production.

Whilst most of these costs would be borne by the supplier, the overall result in supply chain terms is an increase in the total cost of supply, which the supplier would need to recover from future contracts. Therefore your negotiations with suppliers and customers to resolve the variation in supply should aim not to establish blame, but to identify the cause and reduce the likelihood of future variations.

However, where suppliers are unco-operative, or you have suffered loss as a result of variations, you may need to consult your legal advisers about action to obtain redress. Variations and their resolution should be recorded in the vendor rating system and communicated to customers and relevant managers.

Where supplier performance consistently fails to match requirements, you may wish to dispense with the supplier, but there may be reasons of supply or contract conditions making this an unattractive option in the short term. New suppliers or suppliers of new products may also be having short-term difficulties, which it is in both their and the customer's interests to overcome through co-operation. This may be achieved through involving the supplier in future supplier development programmes (see Chapter 6), through which assistance with the implementation of agreed changes may be provided.

INVESTIGATE

- *What procedures does your organization have for monitoring deliveries and dealing with variations in supply? Are they efficient and effective? How might the costs of variations be reduced?*

Invoicing and payment

Before progressing an invoice for payment, you need to check that the details are in accord with the purchase order and any delivery note. However, you may wish to develop a system for carrying over minor discrepancies in amounts payable from one invoice to another, in order to avoid the administrative costs of amending the paperwork for the sake of a few pence or pounds. This was a practice which Peter Garnett identified as a means of reducing the cost of purchasing in Glaxo (see Chapter 1).

Once you have confirmed that the order is complete, you need to ensure that full payment is made promptly and in compliance with the payment terms agreed in the contract, especially where you have the opportunity to benefit from discounts for early payment, or to avoid interest on late payment.

Whilst the need to progress deliveries and resolve variations results from a concern about supplier performance to contract, late payment is what concerns the supplier most about the buyer's performance. This has become a political issue recently, as well as one of business ethics.

The Confederation of British Industry (CBI) has agreed a guide to payment for its members to deal with the problem. GEC's Chairman, Lord Prior, was forced to defend the company against complaints of late payment to suppliers at the annual shareholders' meeting in 1994 (*Daily Telegraph*, 3 September 1994). Whilst the GEC directors rejected the claims of late payment, their eagerness to meet the criticisms of shareholders and suppliers indicates their recognition that good business relationships, and possibly the survival of key suppliers, are crucial to their business. However, the financial position of the buyer's organization may lead to deliberate slippage in the payment of bills to ease cash flow. Late payment may also result from slow or inefficient administrative procedures for payment.

The fear of government legislation to enforce prompt payment may also underly the public response of GEC directors, a fear that will no doubt be increased by the recommendation from the European Commission that creditors should have an 'automatic right to interest at commercial rates on overdue debts' (*Times*, 26 August 1994). This is contrary to UK government policy, outlined in the White Paper on Competitiveness (Department of Trade and Industry, 1994), which does not agree that legislation is necessary. However, as the following extract indicates, late payment by government departments is also a problem.

Late payment of suppliers by government departments

The Government's White Paper on competitiveness says departments and agencies may be forced to pay interest on late payments if current delays do not improve.

In his announcement of the White Paper, Michael Heseltine, President of the Board of Trade, says, 'The Government will in future require all departments and their agencies to comply with the CBI prompt payment code and to set out their performance against this in their annual reports.'

Among other things, this code says payment terms should be settled at the outset of a deal and that organizations should pay bills in accordance with such a contract.

The Government has yet to pass any laws forcing departments to pay interest on late payments. But, Mr Heseltine says, 'If there has not been a significant improvement within the next two years, we will reconsider the case for legislation.'

The Competitiveness White Paper says that besides complying with the CBI code, government bodies should publicize arrangements for handling complaints about late payment.

> *Source: 'Departments to follow business practice of prompt payment', Government Purchasing, **Jul./Aug.**, p. 3, 1994*

Whilst legislation may not be welcomed, buyers may benefit from the threat of its introduction in situations where good relations with suppliers, or their prospects of survival, may be damaged by the failure of the accounts department to pay on time. Fostering good relations with finance and accounts staff may help to speed up payments, especially as they may be doing their best to cope with a mass of paperwork rather than deliberately holding up payments.

Contractual claims

Claims may result from total failure to supply or incomplete supply. The latter may relate to genuinely differing interpretations of the product or service to be supplied, possibly as a result of unclear specification, or of the performance of the product or service. Whilst you should make every effort in such situations to resolve your differences with the supplier, in the absence of agreement recourse to legal remedy may be the only option.

In some circumstances the supplier may deliberately breach the contract, because compliance is likely to be more expensive than the damages resulting from legal action, or the liquidated damages stated in the contract terms and conditions. This may arise because of an unforeseen increase in the supplier's costs, or the availability of a more lucrative contract. Good supplier relations is the best means of avoiding such situations, as well as building in flexibility to contracts by providing incentives, as discussed in Chapter 8. However, if you treat your suppliers as dispensable as soon as a cheaper alternative is available, you cannot expect absolute loyalty in return, though of course this does not affect your legal rights in the case of opportunistic breach by the supplier.

Your involvement in contractual claims is likely to be limited to providing information and assistance to legal and financial staff on their validity. In this eventuality it is essential for the circumstances giving rise to the claim to be documented fully. You need to treat particularly carefully claims relating to the organization's liability arising from bought-in supplies or the actions of service contractors which may threaten strategic organizational interests, and should notify senior management immediately they arise.

Summary

This chapter has examined aspects of contract negotiation, placing, monitoring and management. At one level these may be seen as very formal and adversarial processes, with recourse to legal action lurking beneath every exchange between buyer and supplier. The process of contracting may also be very clerical, paper based and tedious, adding little value to the purchasing process, but necessary in order to protect the buying organization, and to comply with internal rules and procedures. However, the process can be much less costly and time consuming if dealing with suppliers with which you have developed good long-term relationships, and a willingness to overcome problems jointly. Then you may benefit from jointly agreed specifications and performance levels, standard contracts which share risks and benefits, electronic data interchange to increase speed and accuracy, and joint mechanisms for resolving disputes and making good any deficiencies. Most buyers probably operate somewhere in between these extremes, but by focusing on the issue of the overall costs to the supply chain, and ultimately your own organization, of the contracting process, you may find ways to adapt formal procedures in order to reduce their cost, without increasing the risk of damaging the organization's interests.

Activities

1
Prepare a report to your Purchasing Manager reviewing the nature of your negotiations with at least two suppliers in relation to positional bargaining and principled negotiation. Identify the features of both which apply, and which approach is the more effective.

2
Write a brief paper reviewing your organization's practice in relation to fixed-price, cost-plus and incentive contracts. You should outline the benefits and risks of using each type of contract, and identify specific areas of supply particularly suitable for incentive contracts.

References and further reading

Allwright, A. D. and Oliver, R. W. (1993) *Buying Goods and Services – A Professional Guide to Contracting including Model Conditions*, Chartered Institute of Purchasing and Supply, Easton
Carlisle, J. A. and Parker, R. C. (1989) *Beyond Negotiation*, Wiley, Chichester
Fisher, R., Ury, W. and Patton, B. (1991) *Getting to Yes*, Business Books/Random Century, London
Griffiths, M. (1994) *Law for Purchasing and Supply*, Pitman, London
Humphreys, P. (1994) 'CCTA model agreements for buying information systems and services', *Purchasing and Supply Management*, **Apr**, 13–17
Sheridan, D. (1990) *Negotiating Commercial Contracts*, McGraw Hill, Maidenhead
Turpin, C. (1989) *Government Procurement and Contracts*, Longman, Harlow

PART FOUR

Purchasing Effectiveness

10 Developing the effectiveness of purchasing operations

Introduction

In the preceding chapters, various ways of improving purchasing performance have been examined. This chapter is concerned with how purchasing performance may be assessed. You may feel that you are doing a good job, but how can you demonstrate this to your manager and colleagues? Your manager may equally feel that the purchasing department is performing well (or not!), but how can this be demonstrated to senior managers, who have a concern for the overall performance of the organization?

The objectives of this chapter are to:

- Identify what is meant by performance for the organization, for purchasing and for the individual buyer.
- Demonstrate the importance of specifying the relationship between corporate and purchasing goals and individual targets.
- Present a framework linking inputs, processes, outputs and outcomes for use in evaluation.
- Distinguish between qualitative and quantitative indicators, and subjective and objective evaluation.
- Identify the roles of stakeholders, such as customers and suppliers, in evaluation.
- Examine targets for individuals' performance.
- Assess financial measures of performance.
- Identify personality attributes, skills and knowledge characteristic of good buyers, and how they may be developed.

What is performance?

In many organizations, there are explicit statements of the organization's strategic mission, goals and objectives. These may be contained in a strategic plan, and are often displayed prominently for both staff and customers to see. Often these are very generalized – for example, many organizations adopted the concept of excellence and characteristics of corporate culture identified by Peters and Waterman (1982):

- The ability to manage ambiguity and paradox.
- A bias for action.
- Closeness to the customer.
- Encouraging autonomy and entrepreneurship.
- Productivity through people.
- A hands-on commitment to products and services.
- A simple form and lean staffing.
- Knowing your business.

In a similar vein, many organizations seek to achieve 'world class' performance by comparing themselves with other organizations which are regarded as the best at what they do. Schonberger (1986) identified the following principles as combining to create world class manufacturing:

- Total quality management.
- Just-in-time delivery.
- Total preventative maintenance.
- Employee involvement.

In the public sector, value for money is often identified as the overriding goal. Although the precise definition of this term varies, it is generally regarded as delivering public services of the requisite standard at the lowest cost to the taxpayer. This of course operates within a framework of political goals and legal constraints, which may supercede the operational goal of value for money in certain circumstances.

Clearly, not all organizations can achieve world class performance, or afford to invest the resources required to carry out extensive comparison of their own performance against world class performers. However, the aspiration to improve performance is crucial to ensuring that performance is effective, and can be a positive motivational factor for individuals and the purchasing department in general.

Why is performance important for purchasing?

Traditionally purchasing has been regarded as a low-status occupation. Whilst levels of professionalism have improved considerably in recent years, and purchasing's contribution to overall organizational performance through the proactive approach outlined in previous chapters is increasingly being recognized, something of an image problem remains. It is vitally important therefore to be able to project and sustain purchasing's image through marketing the purchasing function to both internal and external customers. This is particularly critical because in many organizations purchasing operates as a business unit or profit centre which is required to meet the cost of the service provided through the value added by savings, improvements in quality, better service from suppliers, etc. Levels of performance are increasingly specified in service level agreements between purchasing and its customers, stating the extent of service provided and standards to which purchasing is committed. There is also an increasing degree of competition with other purchasing organizations. For instance, IBM have established a Procurement Services company which offers its expertise to other organizations; government agencies are not 'tied' to their parent department's purchasing, and are free either to buy their own requirements, or use an outside agency. Therefore performance is about survival at the crudest level: if you, or your department, or the organization as a whole, does not perform, then others will be asked to do so.

What is purchasing performance?

Whilst the above examples illustrate overall organizational goals, purchasing goals also need to be identified. These are often stated as the five 'rights':

- Right material.
- Right quality.
- Right place.
- Rght time.
- Right cost.

Whilst these 'rights' provide a concise, easily memorized statement of purchasing's responsibilities, they require both an overall organizational context and a more detailed definition if they are to be usable in practice. They do, however, reinforce the important point that purchasing is not purely about lowest cost, but needs to consider the other factors which all contribute to providing a quality service to the customer.

Organizational goals may provide guidance on which of the factors should predominate. For instance, lowest cost is often regarded as being dominant in the public sector, particularly in competitive tendering for services. In other sectors, such as aerospace and automobile manufacturing, the costs of poor quality in terms of market share and safety are so high that the lowest cost at the specified quality level is the key factor.

It is also important to note that these factors are not independent: improved quality implies higher cost; delivery location and timing may also affect the cost. Furthermore, if the wrong material is purchased or delivered, there will be cost and time consequences in replacing it. Thus there is a need to use such factors in an integrated manner, recognizing the way in which emphasizing one or the other may affect the overall purchase.

Until recently, British Airways related their purchasing goals to the strategic goals of the organization, as part of a process of demonstrating purchasing's contribution to the company's strategic objectives.

Relationship between the strategic and purchasing goals of British Airways

Corporate goals	Purchasing goals
Safe and secure	Ensure quality of materials and services
Financially strong	Minimize full-life costs
Global leader	Exploit world supply market
Service and value	Provide value for money
Customer driven	Respond to changing requirements
Good employer	Motivated and professional staff
Good neighbour	Consider community and environmental factors

Source: Purchasing Policy and Procedures Manual, British Airways (1992)

Now that its strategic role has been established in British Airways, purchasing goals are no longer explicitly linked to specific strategic goals, but form a necessary element in their achievement.

As far as the public sector is concerned, a report prepared for the Central Unit on Procurement (Treasury, 1993) identified the following as characteristics of high performing purchasing organizations:

- Clear procurement strategy.
- Effective management information and control systems.
- Development of expertise.
- A role in corporate management.
- An entrepreneurial and proactive approach.
- Co-ordination.
- Focused efforts.

This report was based on a survey of a number of private sector organizations regarded as achieving a very high level of performance in purchasing, and demonstrates the value of identifying best practice from other, more competitive sectors.

A survey of chief executive officers or presidents of 135 companies in the manufacturing, service and small company sectors was carried out by the

Centre of Advanced Purchasing Studies (CAPS) in the USA (Bales and Fearon, 1993). They identified the following aspects of purchasing's contribution to the firm as very important:

• Maintain ethical standards	94%
• Assure supply of items	93%
• Assure internal customers' satisfaction	87%
• Contain/reduce prices	87%
• Demonstrate professionalism	86%
• Improve/maintain incoming material quality	75%
• Develop supplier partners	70%

INVESTIGATE

• *Does your organization have an explicit statement of goals and objectives? Are these translated into purchasing objectives? If so, do you and your colleagues know what they are? Can you relate them to your own work? If there are no stated goals and objectives, what do you think they should be?*

Evaluation of purchasing performance

Goals and objectives need to be broken down into the standards and targets against which to assess the overall performance of the organization, as well as purchasing's contribution, and that of individual staff. This is essential to ensure that staff and managers at all levels are aware of the levels of performance which they are expected to achieve.

It is, however, crucial to ensure that the right thing is being measured in the right way. This involves identifying criteria against which performance can be assessed and monitored. The following are most commonly applied:

• *Economy*, which relates purely to inputs.
• *Efficiency*, which is the ratio of inputs or processes to outputs, and therefore measures of profitability and productivity are efficiency measures.
• *Effectiveness*, which is the achievement of overall goals, and could therefore subsume other criteria such as excellence, quality, ethicality and innovation.

Against each criterion, specific targets, in the form of quantitative measures or qualitative indicators, may be identified.

Thus goals and objectives need to be linked to targets at the strategy formulation stage, and mechanisms for monitoring performance against those targets established. Figure 10.1 presents a framework which may be

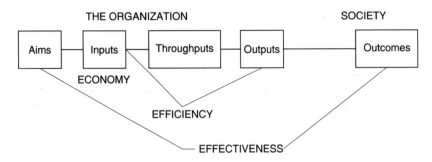

Figure 10.1   Evaluation model

used to relate goals to operational targets, and to ensure that overall performance is being measured, rather than activity for its own sake.

Targets may relate to inputs (staff, expenditure, equipment, etc.), throughputs (the activities which convert inputs, e.g. orders processed), outputs (the immediate products of the processes, e.g. goods or services delivered) and impacts or outcomes (the effects of the outputs on overall organizational performance, e.g. poor-quality parts resulting in lost production or increased maintenance costs).

Understanding the links between what is being measured at each of these stages is critical, as maximizing input or process targets may be at the expense of the output or outcome. It is important therefore to ensure that achievement of short-term targets, such as cutting the cost of the purchasing department by reducing staff numbers (inputs), is not at the expense of long-term targets, such as improving the overall quality of suppliers which will require an extensive programme of supply base analysis.

The above discussion may be related to the level at which the purchasing function is performed, whether clerical, commercial/transactional or strategic. A clerical focus will be purely process oriented, emphasizing measurement of orders placed, backlog of orders to be processed, lead time taken and whether authorization procedures are followed. No consideration will be given to whether the orders processed are actually necessary in relation to overall organizational objectives (outcomes). A commercial focus is still concerned with process, but it is so in relation to the outputs produced or the outcomes sought. Thus targets for savings, delivery, customer service and quality assess either the *efficiency* with which desired outputs are produced, or the *effectiveness* of outputs, for example the impact of improved quality on customer perceptions of the service provided. A strategic focus requires an overview of performance incorporating an operational audit of strategy, organization, systems, benchmarking and customer/supplier analysis.

INVESTIGATE

● *Using the framework presented in Figure 10.1, identify the inputs, processes, outputs and outcomes of your purchasing department. Are the inputs adequate to achieve organizational goals? Could they be achieved with less inputs? Are the processes directed at organizational goals? Could you produce better outcomes with fewer processes, i.e. reduce the numbers of orders processed by rationalizing the supply base?*

Measures and indicators of purchasing performance

A distinction was made above between performance measures and indicators. Measures are generally expressed in figures, and tend to assess performance in areas which are easily measurable, e.g. cost and number of inputs, numbers of orders processed, time taken from requisition to order delivery, financial ratios, savings performance, or numbers of incorrect deliveries, either of time, location or quantity. Whilst such measures are relatively easy to obtain and monitor, in the light of the above discussion, it should be noted that these tend to measure economy and efficiency rather than effectiveness, and therefore emphasize a clerical and commercial, rather than a strategic, focus. Measures therefore should be combined with indicators which are generally expressed in qualitative terms, and are often subjective, i.e. opinions of customers or suppliers on the level of service provided by purchasing staff.

Quantitative measures are more appropriate where the nature of the task is clear, and sets of objective measures that are commonly used in the organization or the sector can be applied with little or no amendment. This is often referred to as 'benchmarking'. A good example are the purchasing benchmarks produced by the Centre for Advanced Purchasing Studies, which are available by sector. Examples from the US transportation sector are illustrated in Box 10.1. Measures need to be clear and easy to understand. Such measures facilitate comparisons between different purchasing departments in large organizations, between similar kinds of organizations, and with competitor companies.

The value of such comparisons may also be seen in the public sector where there are many similar types of organization which are not in competition with each other, e.g. local authorities and NHS authorities, whose performance can be assessed and ranked according to specified criteria. Price monitoring systems such as the Government Supply Index and the Health Service Supply Index (produced by PI Price Management, London) also provide a comparative picture of organizations' performance against this key indicator.

This method is used extensively by the Audit Commission and the National Audit Office. Organizations performing poorly against key indicators may be asked to explain the causes, which may perhaps be due to

Box 10.1 *Summary of the transportation purchasing benchmarks*

The benchmarks are based on data supplied by 29 of the largest US-based transportation companies. Average sales were US$3 billion. In all instances, 'purchases' refers to purchases made through the purchasing department.

Twenty-one purchasing benchmarks were calculated for the 29 transportation companies and for each industry group. Four additional benchmarks were calculated for the airline group only; two additional benchmarks were calculated for the motor carrier group only; and two additional benchmarks were calculated for the railroad group only. More complete data on each of the benchmarks follow, including industry and group benchmarks. In summary:

1 Purchasing (the dollars spent with vendors) accounted for 26% of sales revenue
2 Goods purchases accounted for 11.8% of sales; services purchases accounted for 3.3% of sales; fuel purchases accounted for 10.7% of sales
3 The expense of operating the purchasing function was 17/100 of a cent per dollar of sales
4 It costs about 65/100 of a cent to purchase a dollar of goods or services
5 There was one purchasing employee for every 380 company employees
6 There was one purchasing employee for each US$46 million of sales
7 There were US$11.9 million of purchasing department purchases per purchasing employee
8 Each professional purchasing employee managed US$23.7 million of purchases
9 There were 83 active suppliers per purchasing employee; 10 active suppliers accounted for 90% of all purchases per purchasing employee
10 Each professional purchasing employee managed 166 active suppliers; 20 of these active suppliers accounted for 90% of purchases
11 The value of a purchase order was US$8337
12 Each supplier received US$143 214 of purchasing department purchases
13 For each active supplier, it cost US$933 to operate the purchasing department
14 Of all active suppliers, 19% received 90% of company purchase dollars
15 During the 1-year reporting period, the number of active suppliers increased by 0.77%
16 Minority-owned businesses received 7.1% of total purchases
17 Women-owned businesses received 3.0% of all purchases
18 Electronic data interchange (EDI) using ANSI X12 Standard (excluding FAX) was used to process 12.4% of company purchase dollars; 17.9% of all line items; and 10.2% of all transactions
19 The purchasing department made 86% of the total goods purchases; 45% of the total services purchases; and 72% of all fuel purchases
20 After a purchase request was received in the purchasing department, it took 6.1 days for a supplier to receive a purchase order
21 Requisitions are processed on-line by 46% of all firms; of these companies using an on-line requisition system, 74% of their requisitions are processed on-line

Airline group
22 EDI with SPEC 2000 Standard was used to process 17% of all transactions
23 Of all active suppliers, 3.5% used EDI with SPEC 2000 Standard
24 Of all firms, 40% had an international purchasing group. Out of those firms with an international purchasing group, 25% are located at a foreign on-site location, and 75% are located within centralized purchasing
25 Of all firms, 60% had a logistics/traffic management department

Motor carrier group
26 Of the total number of transactions processed, 21% were automated (computerized)
27 The average cost to process a purchase order manually was US$27

Railroad group
28 Travel and entertainment accounted for 3.3% of purchasing operating expense
29 Of total purchase dollars spent, 33% were covered by long-term purchase agreements (of 6 months or longer)

Source: Centre for Advanced Purchasing Studies, Tempe, Arizona, USA

special demographic circumstances. An example relating to NHS supplies is presented below.

A core set of 18 quantitative indicators were used in 1991–92. These covered purchasing expenditure, operational costs, stock value, stock turn, ratios of staff cost to operational cost and purchasing expenditure, service levels, and prices paid for selected items (NHS Management Executive (1991) *Supplies Indicators and Data Collection Manual*). One of the indicators is the 'overall service level of supplies-controlled stores', which is defined as the 'number of requisition lines satisfied as a percentage of the number requested in the period' on a quarterly basis. Figure 10.2 shows the performance of the NHS regions against this indicator, showing clearly those with below average performance.

By themselves, the data in Figure 10.2 have little significance in relation to overall performance of the NHS regions, but they do provide the basis for asking why some regions seem to be performing poorly. However, should a pattern emerge over a couple of years and across the range of indicators, then more serious investigation and corrective action may be necessary. There will also be the opportunity for identifying and spreading best practice from those regions with a high level of performance.

One important limitation of this approach is that the indicators are internal to the NHS. There is no comparison with private health service providers, or with other comparable sectors or industries. This may be carried out as a separate exercise, in order to ensure that the required standard of performance is not set at too low a level.

Figure 10.2 is a purely quantitative indicator, although it could be argued that it is the service level perceived by the customer, rather than the number of requests met, which is important.

Qualitative indicators are more appropriate in situations where there may be different perspectives on or uncertainty about the nature of the task. Thus the perceptions of stakeholders are sought through interviews or questionnaire surveys with the aim of achieving a consensus on what constitutes good performance and hence the criteria against which the organization or function is to be assessed.

These methods may be, and often are, combined with qualitative methods being used for a strategic evaluation of overall organizational or departmental performance, and quantitative methods for commercial evaluation applied at the level of the buying team or individual, or to assess the overall productivity of the function.

INVESTIGATE

- *What qualitative indicators and quantitative measures are used to assess the performance of your purchasing department? Are there industry standard benchmarks which are applicable?*

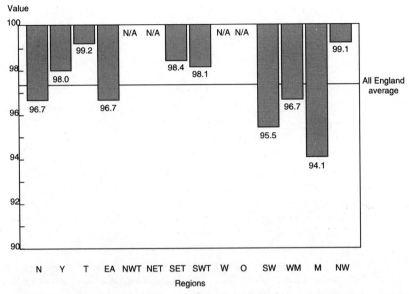

Figure 10.2 NHS performance indicator: service levels (April–June 1991) (From NHS Information Systems Directorate, Supplies Indicators, January–June 1991, April–June 1991, NHS Management Executive, Reading)

A detailed methodology for carrying out such an evaluation in the purchasing context is provided by Ruch and Hendrick (1988). It comprises the following stages:

- Identify stakeholders: buyers, purchasing supervisors and managers, internal customers and suppliers.
- Select a small number of participants who are reasonably representative of each group of stakeholders.
- Generate criteria for evaluation (the group identified 188 criteria).
- Select the 20 most important criteria.
- Each group weights the criteria in order of importance, and selects those highest rated.
- Each group is then weighted in importance (the weights allocated were: customers 34%, buyers 26%, managers 26%, suppliers 14%).
- Select the 10 most highly rated criteria to be used after multiplying the groups' selections by their weight: five objective and five subjective criteria resulted which are listed below with their percentage weights.
- Establish quantified values for each objective indicator against which to rate performance. For example, on-time delivery of 96% was rated super, 90% good, 83% average and 69% poor (incidentally, these seem rather generous to suppliers!).
- Establish qualitative ratings (scale 1–5) for the subjective criteria.

The criteria selected and their percentage weightings were as follows:

• On-time delivery	24%
• Incoming quality assurance acceptance	20%
• Actual versus target cost	11%
• Commodity knowledge	10%
• Purchase order cycle time	7%
• Cultivates qualified suppliers	7%
• Workmanship error rate	6%
• Knows the bottom price	5%
• Commodity complexity	5%
• Timely response to enquiries	5%
Total	100%

The weights enable an overall assessment of effectiveness to be made which distinguishes between those criteria which are critical to success, and those which are of lesser importance.

Whilst the approach may be criticized for depending heavily on the selection of a representative sample of participants, and as being too complicated in terms of assigning quantitative weights to participants and criteria, it is a model which may be applied effectively in a less sophisticated form to any purchasing department. Try applying it to your own area of work, and see how well you are performing!

INVESTIGATE

• *Purchasing audit is another method by which the various components of purchasing performance may be assessed in an integrated manner. Box 10.2 provides a checklist of questions against which the function may be assessed. See how your own department performs using this approach.*

Evaluation of individuals' performance

In many organizations, purchasing goals are translated into individual performance targets which may form part of annual appraisals and contribute to assessment of performance related pay. Targets may be specified in job descriptions. In British Airways, key result areas (KRAs) are set for all staff, including directors. KRAs should be:

• Measurable.
• Achievable.
• Realistic.
• Challenging.

Box 10.2   *Questionnaire used for purchasing audit*

1   Is the purchasing department within your company subject to regular audit by: Yes ☐   No ☐
    (a) External auditors?   Yes ☐   No ☐
    (b) Internal auditors?   Yes ☐   No ☐
    (c) A central purchasing function?   Yes ☐   No ☐
    (d) A purchasing research function?   Yes ☐   No ☐
    (e) External consultants?   Yes ☐   No ☐
    (f) Any other party? (Please specify)   Yes ☐   No ☐

2   If you have answered YES to any parts of question 1, with what frequency is your purchasing department audited?
    (a) Every 6 months?   ☐
    (b) Every 12 months?   ☐
    (c) Every 2 years?   ☐
    (d) Some other frequency? (Please specify)   ☐
    (e) On an irregular basis?   ☐

3   If you have answered YES to question 1, please complete the following table indicating with a tick or a cross in the appropriate box IN THE FIRST COLUMN whether the audit covers the areas described, and IN THE SECOND COLUMN whether in your professional opinion the audit is thorough in the way it covers the area described:

    Does the audit ensure that:
    (a) Company authority levels are observed?   ☐   ☐
    (b) A documentary trail exists from requisition to invoice?   ☐   ☐
    (c) High value orders are supported by competitive bids?   ☐   ☐
    (d) Laid down purchasing policies and procedures are followed?   ☐   ☐
    (e) User quality levels are challenged to prevent overspecification?   ☐   ☐
    (f) Purchasing pursues an active policy of market sourcing?   ☐   ☐
    (g) Purchasing has an objective basis for source selection?   ☐   ☐
    (h) Purchasing conducts thorough supplier appraisal programmes?   ☐   ☐
    (i) The company is protected by an adequate degree of contractual safeguards in its
        dealing with suppliers?   ☐   ☐
    (j) The purchasing department operates effective management of prices?   ☐   ☐
    (k) The purchasing department operates effective quality management techniques?   ☐   ☐
    (l) The purchasing department operates effective delivery management techniques?   ☐   ☐
    (m) The purchasing department seeks to reduce quoted prices by negotiation?   ☐   ☐
    (n) The purchasing department has an active cost-reduction programme?   ☐   ☐
    (o) The purchasing department has an effective system for disposing of surplus
        material and equipment?   ☐   ☐
    (p) The purchasing department has an ongoing programme of identifying areas of
        vulnerability?   ☐   ☐

4   If you answered YES to question 1, is the audit used primarily (select ONE option only):
    (a) As part of a review of financial control within the company?   ☐
    (b) As part of a review of managerial control within the company?   ☐
    (c) As a means of measuring purchasing performance?   ☐
    (d) As an *ad hoc* tool to investigate specific problems?   ☐

5   If you answsered NO to question 1, how is the performance of your purchasing department measured? (Select as many options as are relevant, and rank them in order of importance, i.e. 1 = most important, 5 = least important):
    (a) In comparison with previous performance?   ☐ (   )
    (b) In comparison with targets or standards?   ☐ (   )
    (c) In comparison with other companies or other divisions of same company?   ☐ (   )
    (d) By cost savings made?   ☐ (   )
    (e) By some other method? (Please specify)   ☐ (   )

Source: Used in the research for E. Evans and B. G. Dale, 'The use of audits in purchasing', International Journal of Logistics and Materials Management, *18, 7, 1989*

All KRAs will reflect the overall company and departmental strategic goals but will contain Specific Key Results, the detailed objectives and deliverables for the individual. This is equally true for senior management as for other staff, although the Specific Key Results for managers are likely to reflect more strategic projects and initiatives rather than simple cost performance or process based targets. In addition to targets agreed for each section, each member of staff will have individual goals, such as developing a contract with an individual supplier or representing purchasing on a task force. Performance is assessed through the staff appraisal system, with each KRA being rated in terms of its degree of challenge, and staff performance rated from unacceptable to outstanding. An example of KRAs is presented below. Whilst the savings targets presented below are expressed in terms of price performance, British Airways are now implementing measures of savings based on whole life costs.

Key result areas, Chief Buyer, British Airways

1   Meeting the Business Targets

   - 15% Cost avoidance target
   - 10% Direct savings target on appropriate spend
   - Implement new price increase assessment system including industry checklist
   - Maintain price increases within levels identified on industry checklist.

2   Initiate Business Development
   - Initiate and manage major review of contract staff and consultancy procurement:
      (a) Increase usage of preferred suppliers
      (b) Investigate ways of simplifying ordering of contract staff
      (c) Explore Third World opportunities for software development and report
   - Establish issues to be addressed and process followed concerning the letting of business to company X:
      (a) Agree communication methods and programme and actively support Commercial Manager (company X) in policy debate with relevant parties
   - Analyse the commercial status and direction of Crew Business Centre and test understanding with General Manager, Business Centres
   - Measure and control demands of subsidiary companies
   - Co-ordinate and agree policy with Information Management (IM).

3   Manage the Supplier Base

- Formulate ways better to control supplier activities within IM Business Centres (IMBCs):
  (a) Specifically track activities of (major information technology (IT) companies) in IM purchasing systems and feed information into IM operations
  (b) Investigate ways of establishing likely future purchases of standard hardware and software and feed results into IM operations
- Improve market knowledge of staff within Business Centre Purchasing (BCP):
  (a) All Purchasing Executives (PEs) to visit at least one supplier per month. Supplier analysis checklist to be produced. Visit reports to be held on new central database.

4 Reduction of Inefficiency within Own Section
  - Enhance usage of IT systems where appropriate:
    (a) Ensure correct use and understanding (of internal systems)
    (b) Each PE to undertake detailed investigation and report on potential for improved utilization of existing IT systems
  - Conduct task rating exercise within BCP concentrating on input versus added value. Specifically:
    (a) Research detailed work flows within section; define key areas/activities for rationalization; propose solution and implementation plan
  - Review location of Information Management Purchasing with IMP management team concentrating on centralized versus decentralized issues and report.

5 Forge Improved Links with Clients
  - Forge increasingly sound and relaxed personal/professional relationships with senior IM managers; specifically Business Centre General Managers and their direct reports.

6 Staff Development.

7 Self-development.

Source: Reproduced by kind permission of British Airways

The range of activities covered is significant. In terms of the approach adopted in this book, there are KRAs relating to analysing the market, supplier appraisal and optimizing the supplier base by increasing the use of preferred suppliers. Then there are a range of indicators relating to the contracting process, including planning requirements, improving the efficiency of administrative processes, as well as a strong emphasis on savings targets. There is a mixture of quantitative measures, such as cost avoidance and savings targets, as well as qualitative indicators such as developing better relationships with clients. In addition, the KRAs are concerned not just with economy (savings) and efficiency (improving work flows), but with overall effectiveness. This is especially so in respect of improved service to clients and staff development. Thus the KRAs collectively do relate to overall performance, rather than a narrow perception based solely on reducing input price or ordering processes.

INVESTIGATE

- *Do you have individual performance targets? Do they reflect overall purchasing goals of the organization? Do the measures which are used to assess performance actually relate to the achievement of strategic goals, rather than purely clerical processes?*

Financial measures of performance

In the CAPS survey of chief executive officers and presidents discussed earlier in this chapter, the area where purchasing was perceived as adding the greatest value was in contributing to the firm's bottom-line profit. Whilst from the above discussion it is clear that no single measure can fully reflect overall performance, in practice organizations will expect you to be able to quantify your financial contribution in terms of savings performance.

However, the definition of savings performance is by no means clear cut. The Central Unit on Procurement (1989) defines various aspects of savings performance as follows:

- *Price savings*: the amount by which the last price paid is reduced.
- *Price avoidance*: the amount by which a supplier's price increase request is reduced aiming towards a zero increase.
- *Price increase*: the amount by which the last price paid is increased.

You may wish at this point to refer back to Chapter 6 where a distinction was made between price and cost. The above measures relate purely to the price requested by the supplier, and may bear no relation to the costs of production. These measures also tell you nothing about the nature of the market: if it is highly competitive, then price savings may be a useful indicator, but otherwise the initial price request is likely to be inflated. Thus, even if it is reduced after negotiation, the buyer could still be paying over the odds for the prevailing market conditions.

- *Equivalent financial saving*: a saving which is not based on movement in price, and therefore is less easily quantifiable – examples include savings which result from elimination of, or change in requirements stated by end-users; change in specifications; substitution of lower cost items including refurbished items or items surplus elsewhere; extended payment terms; extended warranty; improved operational efficiency; lower administrative costs.

In calculating price savings, care should also be taken to ensure that the whole-life costs of the purchase are considered, rather than the immediate purchasing price alone (see Chapter 8). Thus factors such as costs of maintenance, estimated working life, residual values, efficiency of operation, etc., should be taken into account in respect of high value products with an extended working life.

Syson (1992, pp. 241-4) suggests a number of price comparisons which may be used to assess buying performance:

- *Sectoral/product retail price index (RPI)*: whilst this provides a general comparator, it only indicates performance against an average, and does not challenge the baseline of costs to which the inflation is added.
- *Price indices*: these are open to similar criticism but, as the best examples, such as the Purchasing Index, relate to actual prices paid for specific products, they are more directly related to standard industry practice.
- *Price against market*: this relates the price to be paid to suppliers to what it is expected the market will bear in terms of a selling price. The buyer is assessed by the variance up or down from budgeted price.
- *Price against suppliers' costs*: this is the most sophisticated and strategically oriented measure, as it seeks to relate price paid to the supplier's actual costs. It therefore implies the sort of strategic partnership relationship discussed in Chapter 5, where there is sharing of financial information between supplier and buyer. Through supplier development activities (Chapter 6) some of the supplier's costs may be expected to reduce, and therefore buyers will be judged on what level of reductions they can achieve, rather than how low an increase may be.

INVESTIGATE

- *What savings related measures are used in your organization?*

Improving individual performance

So far in this chapter we have examined ways of assessing the performance of the purchasing department and the individuals within it. However, from a personal point of view, you may wish to consider what characteristics a good buyer has. This is clearly a very important issue for all organizations, as well as those working or aspiring to a career in the function. If an organization can identify the attributes of individuals who are more likely to become successful buyers, then a high level of performance should in principle be easier to achieve and maintain. Equally, on an individual level, if you are considering a career in purchasing, you will wish to consider whether you have the right mix of personality attributes, skills and knowledge to succeed. If you are an experienced buyer, you should also consider the need to obtain new skills and knowledge in order to keep up with changes in the profession and the businesses and public sector organizations it serves.

However, establishing a definitive set of attributes, skills and knowledge is by no means an exact science. Therefore if you do not match up to the following sets of attributes, or feel deficient in skills and knowledge, do not despair! The lists presented below are collections of attributes, skills and knowledge which no individual possesses in totality, but which are amalgamations of those identified by practitioners as being characteristic of successful buyers. Equally, it is impossible to say, without considerable further research, which individual attributes, skills and knowledge are critical, and which are merely desirable. Furthermore, every situation may demand different sets of attributes, skills and knowledge. Thus the following lists are presented purely for information, and as a checklist to assess how you match up, with the above limitations in mind.

Personality attributes, skills and knowledge

The first set is taken from evidence collected during the research carried out for the development of the purchasing National and Scottish Vocational Qualifications (NVQs and SVQs) (see Chapter 1). All attributes, skills and knowledge mentioned at least once by any interviewee are included. The exact words used by practitioners are reproduced to give a flavour of individuals' own perceptions, rather than rephrasing or categorizing them. See how you rate against them. Against each attribute, skill or area of knowledge indicate whether it applies to you to a high, medium or low extent.

Personality attributes

Attribute	High	Medium	Low
Politician	☐	☐	☐
Confidence	☐	☐	☐
No ego	☐	☐	☐
Leader	☐	☐	☐
In charge	☐	☐	☐
Talk to people	☐	☐	☐
Listener	☐	☐	☐
Assertive	☐	☐	☐
Initiative	☐	☐	☐
Deal maker	☐	☐	☐
Empathy	☐	☐	☐
Persuasiveness	☐	☐	☐
Team worker	☐	☐	☐
Consultant	☐	☐	☐

Some of the attributes mentioned are somewhat obscure: being a 'politician' could hide a multitude of sins, for instance. There are also some contradictions in the above list, e.g. it is difficult to reconcile a buyer having 'no ego', but at the same time having 'confidence' and being 'in charge'. There are, however, a mixture of active, forceful attributes ('assertive' and 'leader') and of passive ones ('listener' and 'empathy') suggesting that the successful buyer must be able to play both roles, as circumstances demand. The idea of the buyer as a 'deal maker' suggests that an aptitude for bargaining and fashioning an agreement which suits all parties is important.

Skills

Skill	High	Medium	Low
Communication	☐	☐	☐
Literacy	☐	☐	☐
Numeracy	☐	☐	☐
Computers	☐	☐	☐
Assimilate information	☐	☐	☐
Negotiation strategy	☐	☐	☐
Risk management	☐	☐	☐
Building relationships	☐	☐	☐
Planning, monitoring and reviewing	☐	☐	☐
Team work	☐	☐	☐
Problem solving	☐	☐	☐
Marketing the purchasing function	☐	☐	☐
Playing internal politics	☐	☐	☐
Recognizing non-verbal clues	☐	☐	☐
Good memory	☐	☐	☐
Ability to think on your feet	☐	☐	☐

Many of the above skills relate to communication ('building relationships', 'recognizing non-verbal clues' and 'team work') and 'soft' interpersonal skills, whilst others relate to 'hard' skills such as literacy, numeracy and computers. The balance between them any individual possesses will obviously vary, and some buyers will be happier with regular direct interaction with suppliers and hard negotiations, whilst others may prefer planning, financial analysis and working with computers. Ideally, though, all buyers should be able to demonstrate both sets of skills when necessary.

Knowledge

Subject	High	Medium	Low
Market	☐	☐	☐
Product	☐	☐	☐
Production processes	☐	☐	☐
Business functions	☐	☐	☐
Accountancy	☐	☐	☐
Suppliers	☐	☐	☐
Buying options	☐	☐	☐
Contract terms and conditions	☐	☐	☐
Suppliers' costs	☐	☐	☐
Legal	☐	☐	☐
Ethical	☐	☐	☐
Resources required	☐	☐	☐

The above list contains both knowledge that is specific to the function and organization, such as 'market', 'suppliers' and 'contract terms and conditions', as well as general areas of knowledge, such as 'business functions', 'accountancy' and 'legal'. In many organizations a feature of staff development programmes for trainee buyers is a period of work in departments other than purchasing. As purchasing is increasingly seen as a strategic function from which future senior managers will emerge, on the same standing as finance, production or marketing, clearly the need to possess and develop generally applicable business knowledge increases. However, the importance of the knowledge of markets and suppliers which the buyer uniquely possesses should not be underestimated, and should give you an advantage over those from other functions, as well as enhancing the organization's overall performance if it is deployed at a strategic level.

Some support for the above listings is provided in research carried out in 1984 in the USA, suggesting that many of the attributes, skills and knowledge are not subject to substantial change over time or geographical location (Moore et al., 1984). In addition to specific competences which contain many of those listed above, Moore et al. summarized additional characteristics of good buyers as follows:

- 'Understand how to plan, organize and control purchasing activities'.

- 'Need to be analytically oriented, moderately aggressive, able to perceive things from a holistic perspective, and capable of exercising self-control.'
- 'Understand the importance of a convincing professional appearance, the need for a balanced use of intuition and discretion, and the value of quasi-professional involvement with professional and civic organizations.'

No doubt by now you are feeling somewhat inadequate, as none of us can be expected to match up to such ideal, overall statements of the characteristics of a good buyer. I am not sure whether the following case of a world class buying organization's expectations of its buyers will reassure you, but at least it sets a standard to which we can all aspire. How do British Airways' expectations relate to the above listings of attributes, skills and knowledge?

What British Airways looks for in its buyers

- Rounded individuals
- Personal skills
- Professional expertise

1 *Energy and drive:*
   - strong desire to achieve results
   - willing to work hard and under pressure
   - demonstrate persistence and resilience when faced with difficulties
2 *Good communicators:*
   - good listener, remains open minded and understands the views of others
   - respond positively when challenged, take it on
   - present business case for additional resources
   - negotiate with and influence outside suppliers and client areas
   - deal with overt conflict
3 *Team players:*
   - able to handle involvement with a variety of people at different levels within and outside the organization
   - can work closely with others to achieve a common goal
4 *Good decision maker:*
   - able to work on your own and take calculated risks, making tough commercial decisions under pressure affecting staff in own and supplier companies
   - able to sift information and analyse data to support decisions
   - highly numerate

5   *Good planner and organizer:*
   – deal with different aspects of managing business, from coun-
     selling staff to major internal/external negotiation
   – able to prioritize and develop plans making optimum use of
     available resources
   – flexibility to adapt to changing business environment
6   *Innovation:*
   – generates own ideas to improve supply of goods and/or ser-
     vices and efficiency of own function
   – prepared to try out new ideas and accommodate construc-
     tive challenges
7   *Strategic awareness:*
   – understanding of corporate aims and application to own
     function
8   *Self awareness:*
   – able to appraise own performance and learn from experience

Source: Reproduced by kind permission of British Airways

The above characteristics relate mainly to personality and skills, though the latter clearly depend on knowledge. Personality attributes such as 'listener', 'empathy', 'initiative' and 'team worker' are supported, as are the following skills: 'communication', 'literacy', 'numeracy', 'ability to assimilate information', 'negotiation strategy', 'risk management', 'planning, monitoring and reviewing', 'team work' and 'problem solving'. In addition, however, some hard-edged commercial attributes and skills are sought: ability to 'deal with overt conflict', to 'work on your own and take calculated risks', and to 'make tough commercial decisions affecting staff in own and supplier companies'.

Developing your skills and knowledge to improve effectiveness

The fact that you are reading this book suggests that you are already registered for NVQ or SVQ assessment or for a course of study at a college or university, which in turn may lead to formal recognition by a professional body. Thus you have recognized the need to acquire new skills and knowledge or update those you have developed and practised over many years of experience. It is hoped that this book will prove sufficient to meet your requirements in respect of those purchasing skills and knowledge identified above which are directly related to the sourcing and contracting functions.

Ethical knowledge was cited in the NVQ and SVQ research, and the CAPS survey referred to above identified 'maintaining ethical standards' as purchasing's most important contribution to the firm. There is a requirement in many of the purchasing Elements of competence to conduct relations with others in a professional manner, in which ethics clearly plays an important part. The ethical code of the Chartered Institute of Purchasing and Supply (CIPS) is available on request (for the address, see Further information at the end of this chapter), and there are occasionally journal articles on the subject (see for instance Robson (1993) and Arkinstall (1994)).

Generic skills such as numeracy, literacy, communication, team work, maintaining good relationships, and problem solving are embedded within the NVQ and SVQ Elements of competence to which they are relevant, and are not considered directly in this text. However, there are many texts to which you may refer if you feel you need to improve your skills and knowledge in these areas, some of which are listed in the References and further reading given at the end of this chapter.

Your own organization may have staff development programmes which cover most of the areas identified above, and which you may access in order to fill any skill or knowledge gaps which become apparent from your assessment for the purchasing NVQ or SVQ. Many organizations are now developing competence based training programmes. Some, such as Rolls Royce Aerospace, make use of the NVQ and SVQ competences; others, such as London Underground and Shell, identify competences which relate to their own organizational context. The Civil Service has developed a Certificate and Diploma of Competence for staff of government departments and agencies which carries exemption from parts of the CIPS professional qualifications.

CIPS have also recognized the NVQ and SVQ routes to professional qualification. On satisfactory completion of the Level 4 qualification, submission of a portfolio of evidence, completion of a project and a final interview, candidates will be accepted as full members.

Should you wish to obtain an academic qualification, many colleges and universities now offer Business and Technology Education Council, degree and postgraduate courses in purchasing, in some cases as an option on a general business studies course. CIPS recognize many such courses for exemption from parts of their professional qualifications, as well as offering preparation for their own professional examinations through many colleges. A list of institutions offering such courses is available from CIPS.

If you are interested in keeping up with developments in academic research, you may wish to join the International Purchasing and Supply Education and Research Association (IPSERA), of which purchasing practitioners as well as academics from many countries are members. IPSERA holds an annual conference as well as several workshops each year, and maintains a research database designed to put people with similar research interests and real world organizational problems in touch with each other. The contact address is listed under Further information at the end of this chapter.

Qualifications are of course only the outward sign of attainment, recognized by an accredited awarding body. Only you and, to a lesser extent, your colleagues and managers, really know how well you match up in terms of the competences, knowledge and skills required in your job, today and as it develops in the future. Personal effectiveness lies in recognizing any deficiencies at an early stage and rectifying them, and in keeping up with developments in the body of knowledge and practice within the profession to be able to cope with change, rather than be overwhelmed by it.

Summary

From the above it should be clear that achieving excellence in purchasing is a multifaceted task, and achievement may be interpreted subjectively by senior managers and other stakeholders in different ways in different organizations. Equally, it may be evaluated using both quantitative and qualitative measures and indicators, at various levels within the organization, strategic, departmental, buying team and individual. Whilst there is substantial experience and a wide range of sources on operational measures, strategic evaluation of the contribution of purchasing to overall organizational goals is less well developed. From the above discussion, however, this is clearly a critical area, and one by which, increasingly, the value of the purchasing function, and your own work, will be judged. Finally, personality attributes, skills and knowledge areas which have been identified as characteristic of good buyers are presented, together with sources of information and courses through which you may continue to develop your personal and professional effectiveness.

Activities

1   Your Purchasing Manager has asked you to review the way in which the performance of the purchasing department is assessed. You should identify what clerical, commercial and strategic measures and indicators are currently used, and recommend ways in which the assessment of the overall effectiveness of the department may be improved.

2   Using Ruch and Hendrick's methodology, identify criteria against which to assess the performance of the purchasing department, and establish your rating against each criterion.

References and further reading

Adams, F. P. and Niebuhr, R. E. (1985) 'Improving individual productivity in purchasing', *Journal of Purchasing and Materials Management*, **21**(4), 2–8

Arkinstall, D. (1994) 'Ethics in practice – What is acceptable to the buyers of tomorrow?, *Purchasing and Supply Management*, **Oct.**, 12–13

Bales, W. A. and Fearon, H. E. (1993) *CEOs' and Presidents' Perceptions and Expectations of the Purchasing Function*, Centre for Advanced Purchasing Studies, Arizona State University

Broadbent, M. and Cullen, J. (1993) *Managing Financial Resources*, Butterworth-Heinemann, Oxford

Evans, E. F. and Dale, B. G. (1989) 'The use of audits in purchasing', *International Journal of Logistics and Materials Management*, **18**, 7, 15–23

Hughes, B. (1992) 'Purchasing Charter: goals per world class purchasing', *Purchasing and Supply Management*, **Mar.**, 37–38

Moore, J. M., Luft, R. L. and Eckrich, D. W. (1984) 'A hierarchy of purchasing competences', *Journal of Purchasing and Materials Management*, **Spring**, 8–14

Murdock, A. and Scutt, C. (1993) *Personal Effectiveness*, Butterworth-Heinemann, Oxford

Northedge, A. (1990) *The Good Study Guide*, Open University, Milton Keynes

Peters, T. and Waterman, R. H. (1982) *In Pursuit of Excellence*, Harper Row, New York

Quayle, M. (1990) 'Measuring purchasing performance', *Purchasing and Supply Management*, **Mar.** 28–32

Reck, R. F., Landeros, R. and Lyth, D. M. (1992) 'Integrated supply management: the basis for professional development', *International Journal of Purchasing and Materials Management*, **Summer**, 12–18

Robson, R. (1993) 'Promotions and gifts', *Purchasing and Supply Management*, **Nov.**, 20–21

Ruch, W. A. and Hendrick, T. E. (1988) 'A model for professional productivity: evaluating purchasing performance', *National Productivity Review*, **Autumn**, 285–297

Schonberger, R. (1986) *World Class Manufacturing: The Lessons of Simplicity Applied*, Free Press, New York

Syson, R. (1992) *Improving Purchase Performance*, Pitman, London

Targett, D. (1984) *Coping with Numbers*, Blackwell, Oxford

Thomson, R. (1993) *Managing People*, Butterworth-Heinemann, Oxford

Treasury (1993) *Organisation of Procurement in Government Departments and their Agencies*, HMSO, London

Wilson, D. A. (1993) *Managing Information*, Butterworth-Heinemann, Oxford

Further information

Chartered Institute of Purchasing and Supply, Easton House, Easton on the Hill, Stamford, Lincolnshire PE9 3NZ, UK. Tel. 01780 56777

Phil Southey, Membership Secretary, International Purchasing and Supply Education and Research Association, Coventry University SE-T, Priory Street, Coventry CV1 5FB, UK

Index